AI Ethics, Security, and Governance Demystified

Your Guide to Ethical AI Practices for a Safer Tomorrow

Madhusmita P. Patil
Kapila Arora
Gaurav Aroraa

ARCCHIE

AI Ethics, Security, and Governance Demystified

Your Guide to Ethical AI Practices for a Safer Tomorrow

Editor: Shambhu
Production Manager: Gaurav Mutreja
Cover design by Freepik and Vecteezy
Formatting & Indexing: Rahul

First Edition: Feb-2025
Reference: 2408122
Published by Arcchie Publications

ISBN-13 (paperback): 978-81-979768-7-2
ISBN-13 (eBook): 978-81-979768-8-9

Published by ARCCHIE PUBLICATIONS, Greater Noida, U.P. -201 306
and Printed at Repro India Ltd., Mumbai

www.arcchieonline.com

DEDICATED TO

To my daughters Akanksha and Aranya, and the future generation with an effort to raise awareness about the potential of artificial intelligence and the challenges it presents, urging the responsible use of this powerful technology to shape a brighter future.

- Madhusmita P Patil

To my children, Kannan and Dakshi, who eagerly awaited my next book—may you grow up in a world where AI technology serves humanity in responsible way And to the potential users of AI—innovators, dreamers, and decision-makers—may this book inspire challenges around AI and responsible, secure, and ethical choices, ensuring that AI remains a force for good in our ever-evolving world.

- Kapila Arora

To Deepak Gupta, a friend, mentor, and well-wisher whose positive attitude toward work and life constantly inspires me.

- Gaurav Aroraa

ACKNOWLEDGMENT

Authoring a book is a journey. Without my co-authors' support I would not have been able to succeed in this journey. My sincere thanks to the team at Arcchie Publications for providing me the opportunity and guiding me in this journey to bring this book to fruition. Their dedication, enthusiasm, and unwavering commitment have transformed my vision into a tangible reality. My gratitude to my husband Prakash Patil, my parents, my in-laws, for the constant support and encouragement to dream big and work towards it. I also am grateful to my mentor Enikõ Rózsa for her time, guidance, and critical feedback to shape the book.

Finally, my respect goes out to the readers – both novice and expert – who will embark on this exploration with me. It is with the hope that this book ignites curiosity, expands our horizons, and encourages each one of us to use this technology wisely and effectively.

In the spirit of collaboration and shared learning, this book stands as a tribute to the power of human endeavor. Together, we illuminate the path toward a future fueled by the boundless potential of AI and use the technology in a responsible manner.

- Madhusmita P Patil

I would like to dedicate this book to my husband, Raman Goel, for his continuous guidance, fostering positivity, and motivation.

- Kapila Arora

It's hard to understand things in life when you don't find support. My family is one such support system, and I am the luckiest to have them. I want to thank my wife, Shuuby Aroraa, and my little angel, Aarchi Arora, who permitted me to write and invest time in this book—thanks to the ARCCHIE team. Thanks to Madhusmita P Patil, Kapila Arora, and Enikõ Rózsa. Revising this book was a long journey, with valuable participation and collaboration from reviewers, technical experts, and editors (Shambhu, Gaurav, and Team Alexa). Finally, I would like to thank all the readers who have taken an interest in my book and for their support in making it a reality. Your encouragement has been invaluable.

- Gaurav Aroraa

ABOUT THE AUTHORS

- **Madhusmita P Patil** is a technology leader with over twenty-five+ plus years of experience in software and technology. Her expertise spans Enterprise Architecture & Transformation, Strategy Consulting, with a proven track record of driving and delivering solutions for complex business problems. As an innovator, she has been successful in providing First of a Kind solutions for multiple new areas. With a strong customer-centric approach, she has successfully forged new partnerships and is a trusted advisor for multiple high-profile clients. She also has played a pivotal role in championing diversity in leadership and mentoring women in the tech field. She has collaborated with multiple organizations, and premier education institutions, driving efforts to bridge the skill gap between industry and academia. She is an eminent speaker, recognized as an IBM Master Inventor, has twenty plus patents and thirty plus publications to her credit.

- **Kapila Arora** is a Senior Certified Architect at IBM, having almost 20 years. She is a thought leader in Conversation AI, Enterprise Hybrid and Multi Cloud Architectures, specializing in Application Integration, Data, Infrastructure and Government Blockchain Solution. With extensive exposure to the end-to-end lifecycle of enterprise applications (EA), she holds a remarkable track record of architecting and delivering end to end solutions across various industries and global customers across geographies. She effortlessly embraces new technology with a problem-solving approach. She is an enthusiastic and clear thinker. She has been instrumental in leading Diversity and Women in the tech (WIT) for IBM Financial sector. She has been recognized with Women in the tech (WIT) award by one of Largest UK Bank Engagement. She has been recognized with several awards & recognitions throughout her journey within IBM and Previous Organization.

- **Gaurav Aroraa** is a Microsoft MVP award recipient. He is a Mentor of Change with AIM NITI Aayog, Govt. of India, Business Coach with Business Blaster, Govt of NCT of Delhi, India, and President, Open AI Enth. India. He is a lifetime member of the Computer Society of India (CSI), an advisory member and senior mentor at IndiaMentor, certified as a Scrum trainer and coach, ITIL-F certified, and PRINCE-F and PRINCE-P certified. Gaurav is an open-source developer and a contributor to the Microsoft TechNet community. He has authored books across technologies, including Python Programming Demystified - A Clear and Concise Guide (Arcchie), Prompt Engineering for Beginners: A Comprehensive Guide (Arcchie), and Harness AI's Creative Power to Drive Innovation: Learn & Leverage AI to bring paradigm shift to transform the businesses (Arcchie). Recently, Gaurav has been recognized as a world record holder for writing books in exceptional technologies.

ABOUT THE TECHNICAL REVIEWER

Enikő Rózsa is a Distinguished Engineer and CTO for AI at the Global AI & Analytics Practice of IBM Consulting. This role leverages her expertise in developing innovative AI solutions to drive business outcomes. With an impressive career spanning over three decades, Enikő has mastered the art of multi-platform AI development, consistently delivering revolutionary solutions that propel organizations forward. Her expertise in conversation insights enables organizations to differentiate themselves through consistent and repeatable delivery. She has co-authored a book on 'Effective Conversational AI,' covering strategies for enhancing conversational AI systems, offering insights on performance analytics, iterative optimization, and best practices for delivering seamless and compelling user interactions. Throughout her 30-year career with IBM, Enikő has demonstrated versatility, transitioning from Developer to Usability Architect to Delivery Leader of NLP/Recommender systems and now a Technical Executive. She co-invented and led the production implementation of an ontology-based natural language dialogue system, empowering clients with self-service technical support. Enikő is passionate about solving client challenges and is adept at translating business needs into technologies. She has been publishing several patents in the NLP and Usability domains, showcasing her commitment to innovation and expertise. With deep expertise in Generative AI, Enikő Rózsa drives technical innovation and strategic decision-making in AI-first digital transformations. She possesses an extensive understanding of generative AI architecture, algorithms, and their practical applications, enabling her to guide enterprises in optimizing AI models for real-world use cases. Her insights into the evolving AI landscape ensure organizations can harness cutting-edge advancements while maintaining efficiency and scalability. Committed to Ethics and Responsible AI, Enikő integrates fairness, transparency, and accountability into AI-generated content and decision-making systems. She proactively addresses AI biases and ensures ethical safeguards in Conversational AI and Generative AI applications. Her approach combines regulatory awareness with the best technical practices to build responsible AI systems that maintain trust and integrity in customer interactions. Enikő Rózsa is also recognized as a former World Economic Forum Professional Fellow and a co-author in the AI Governance Alliance Briefing Paper series. Her contributions to the groundbreaking Presidio AI Framework: Towards Safe Generative AI Models paper examine the rapid evolution of generative AI while emphasizing the critical balance between innovation, safety, and ethical considerations. This framework redefines the AI lifecycle by integrating enhanced risk management protocols and advocating a "shift-left" approach, embedding safety measures at earlier stages of AI development. A powerful advocate for multistakeholder collaboration, Enikő's work fosters shared accountability and proactive risk mitigation strategies within AI governance. As a cornerstone publication by the AI Governance Alliance, the Presidio AI Framework lays the foundation for sustained efforts in fostering ethical and responsible AI development. It envisions a future where groundbreaking advancements in AI are seamlessly paired with rigorous safeguards, ensuring safety, trustworthiness, and responsible deployment of AI technologies.

PREFACE

As Artificial Intelligence continues transforming industries and societies, the need for ethical considerations, robust security measures, and effective governance structures has never been more critical. This book comprehensively explores these themes, providing readers with the knowledge and tools to implement responsible AI practices. Through in-depth analysis, case studies, and practical insights, this book guides professionals, academics, and policymakers in navigating the complex challenges of AI ethics, security, and governance.

This book delves into the essential elements of Artificial Intelligence that are reshaping our society and industries. With AI's growing influence, addressing ethical importance, security concerns, and governance structures is imperative. This book offers insights into responsible AI development, explores frameworks for ethical AI, examines security protocols, and discusses governance models. Most importantly, it guides by combining theoretical foundations with practical applications, supporting professionals, academics, and policymakers in navigating the complex landscape of AI.

Let's embark on this journey of learning together.

What's Inside This Book

Chapter 1: Introduction to Artificial Intelligence overviews AI, its history, evolution, and current state.

Chapter 2: The Ethical Implications of AI explores ethical challenges and considerations in AI development and deployment.

Chapter 3: AI Security: Threats and Solutions covers security risks associated with AI and strategies for mitigating them.

Chapter 4: Governance Frameworks for AI explores governance models and frameworks for effective AI management.

Chapter 5: Testing AI solutions for Security, Ethics and Governance explores various perspectives to test and validate a solution that is ethical, secured and align with compliance requirements.

Chapter 6: Building an Ethical AI Culture in Organizations explores emerging trends and future directions in AI ethics, security, and governance.

For Whom This Book Is Intended

This book is designed for:

- Industry professionals and executives
- Policymakers and regulators
- Academic researchers and students
- Technology enthusiasts
- AI developers and practitioners
- No prior AI experience is required; basic understanding of usage of AI application is beneficial

Download the source code and colored images:

To download the source code bundle

and the colored images, please follow the link

OR

scan the QR Code

https://l1nq.com/9788197976872

Errata

At **ARCCHIE Publications**, we are committed to delivering the highest-quality content in all our publications. We follow best practices to ensure the accuracy of our content to provide our readers with indulgent reading experience. We believe and understand that our readers are our best judges, and we always use their input and feedback from time to time to improve human errors, if any, that may occur during the publishing processes involved. We invite you to participate in our errata submission process to ensure our books remain accurate and up to date. Please help us reach out to readers who might have difficulties due to unforeseen errors. Please write to us at ***errata@arcchieonline.com***.

When submitting errata, please include the following information:

- Book Title
- Reference#
- Author(s)
- Page Number
- Description of the Error
- Suggested Correction (if applicable)

The **ARCCHIE Publications** Family highly appreciates your support, suggestions, and feedback.

Sharing Your Perspective and Providing Feedback

Your perspective is invaluable to us, as it helps us enhance our content and gather your feedback. We warmly welcome all forms of feedback. Please feel free to send us an email at **feedback@arcchieonline.com**, mentioning the book title in the subject line of your message.

Book Review Invitation

We kindly invite you to share your thoughts. After you've read and engaged with this book, consider leaving a review on the platform where you acquired it. Your impartial feedback can greatly assist potential readers in making informed decisions. Your reviews provide valuable insights for us at **Arcchie**, helping us better understand your perspectives on our products, and they offer authors the chance to appreciate your feedback on their work.

PIRACY

Should you encounter unauthorized reproductions of our publications in any digital format on the internet, we kindly request your assistance in pinpointing their locations or website sources. Please reach out to us at **copyright@arcchieonline.com** and include a link to the infringing material.

If you possess expertise in a particular subject and wish to participate in the creation or contribution to a book, please visit **authors.arcchieonline.com**. We welcome you and assist you to start your authorship journey with **ARCCHIE PUBLICATIONS**.

TABLE OF CONTENTS

JOIN US ON THE ARCCHIE PUBLICATIONS DISCORD SERVER

Connect with fellow readers, authors, and enthusiasts to discuss all things related to our publications and the exciting world of AI, programming, and learning. Share your insights, ask questions, and engage in vibrant discussions to expand your knowledge and inspire creativity. Take advantage of this opportunity to be part of a dynamic community dedicated to exploring the frontiers of technology and innovation. Join our Discord Server today and be part of the ARCCHIE Publications community!

https://discord.gg/z26SenmpEt

Chapter 1
Introduction to Artificial Intelligence

This chapter primarily focuses on the basics of AI and how this powerful tool can transform various industries or sectors by bringing in a fresh perspective to the age-old business problems involving manual effort.

In this chapter, the following aspects will be covered

- Definition and scope of AI
- Key milestones in AI development
- AI in modern applications

Definition and scope of AI

Artificial Intelligence (Artificial + Intelligence) is derived from the combination of two words "artificial" and "intelligence". As per the Oxford dictionary, AI means something that is made or produced by human beings rather than occurring naturally. So, AI can be termed as a technology that is created by human beings while trying to recreate or reproduce human intelligence. Even if it is a near simulation or duplication of human intelligence the focus should be on building a trusted system that is contextual and built for a specific purpose without misusing the benefits of technology. Hence, AI can be defined as the application of technology or a software program, i.e. trustworthy, built for purpose, designed and developed to solve a business problem like how a human being would approach.

The foundation of an AI based solution is always data. The ability of an AI solution to understand data, identify/discover patterns from the data and apply complex models for solving a business problem makes it different and unique from a non-AI software solution. At the same time, due to the flexibility that AI brings in for solving a particular problem, it is prone to data misuse, fabricated or manipulated results which destroy the benefits that it brings in.

While data is core to AI systems, scope or applications of AI is diverse. Hence AI systems can be categorized based on the functionality they offer and the capability that they have.

Categorization of AI systems based on functionalities is further described below.

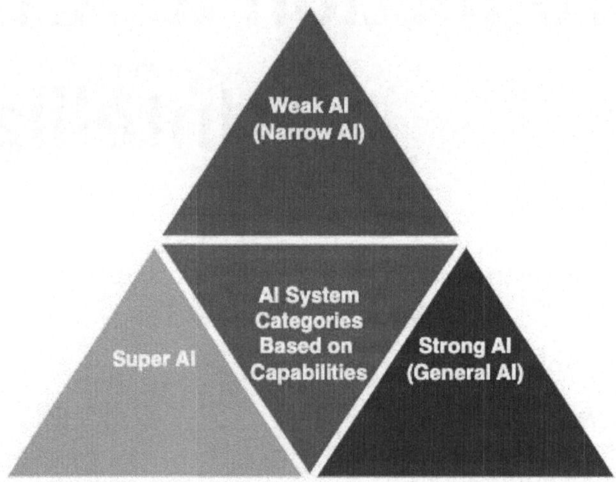

Figure: 1.1 Categorization of AI based on capabilities

- **Weak AI:** Most used AI systems are Weak AI, also referred as Narrow AI. All the other forms of AI are theoretical. This form of AI is mostly trained to perform an individual or small piece of task, much faster and better than a human being. The challenge with this type of AI is in its limitation to perform tasks outside its definition. Virtual assistants, text-based chat systems, google maps are all examples of weak AI.
- **Strong AI:** Strong AI, also known as General AI is more of a theoretical concept. It can use previous learnings and skills to accomplish new tasks in a different context without the need for human beings to train the underlying models. This ability replicates the intellectual task performed by a human being by applying his/her logic.
- **Super AI:** Super AI is commonly referred to as artificial superintelligence and, like strong AI, it is also theoretical. Super AI in a way can be described as an advanced human brain, with more advanced capabilities than strong AI that would include think, reason, learn, make judgements and possess cognitive abilities surpassing those of human beings. It may have capabilities to understand human sentiments and experiences to feel emotions, have

needs and possess beliefs and desires of their own. While Weak AI, Strong AI, Super AI all describe the capabilities of an AI system, AI systems can also be categorized based on functionalities that they support as discussed below.

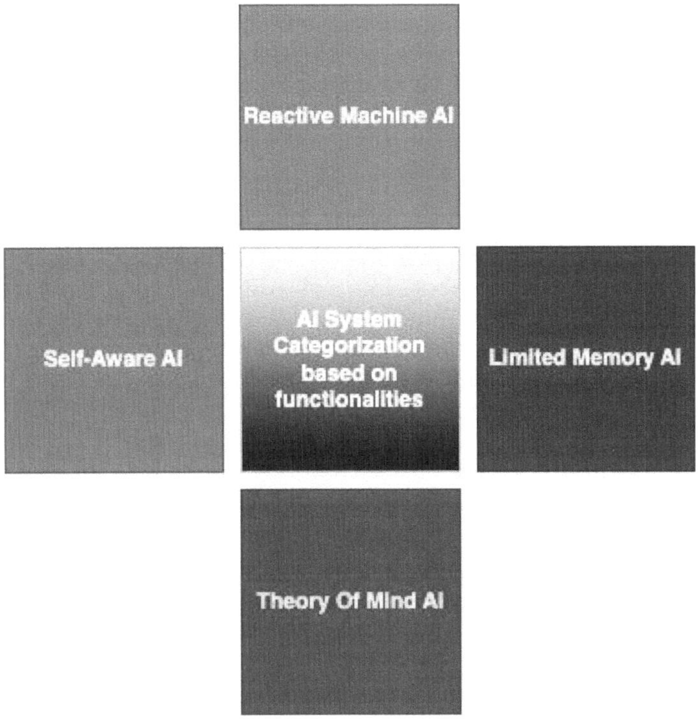

Figure: 1.2 Categorization of AI based on functionalities

Reactive Machine AI

This type of AI system is like Narrow/Weak AI systems. They don't have memory and are designed to perform a very specific task. They do not have the ability to remember previous outcomes or decisions. These are based on current data, use statistical mathematics and can analyze vast amounts of data to produce a seemingly intelligent output. Some popular examples of Reactive Machine AI are

- IBM's chess-playing supercomputer AI, also known as IBM Deep Blue, that beat chess grandmaster Garry Kasparov in the late 1990s by smartly analyzing the pieces on the board and predicting the probable outcomes of each move.
- Netflix's viewing recommendations provide customers with content they're most likely to enjoy, creating a unique experience for the customer. These are solutions powered by models that process data sets collected from viewer's

viewing history to personal choices.

Limited Memory AI

Like Reactive Machine AI, this form of AI also finds its applicability in Narrow AI/Weak AI systems. The only difference between "Limited Memory AI" and "Reactive Machine AI" is that "Limited Memory AI" can recall past events and outcomes and monitor specific objects or situations over time to decide on a course of action most likely to help achieve a desired outcome. However, it has limitations to retain the data in a library of past experiences to use over a long-term period.

- Generative AI tools such as ChatGPT, Bard and Deep AI. These tools possess capabilities to predict the next word, phrase or visual element in the context, within the content it's generating.
- Virtual assistants and chatbots like Siri, Alexa etc. combine natural language processing (NLP) and Limited Memory AI to understand questions and requests, take appropriate actions and compose responses.
- Autonomous vehicles such as self-driving cars understand the world around them in real-time and make informed decisions such as when to speed up, apply brakes, make a turn, etc. based on the trained data and continuity of learning that improves their performance.

Theory of Mind AI

In a way "Theory of Mind AI" can be mapped to a combination of Strong AI and Super AI. This form of AI is theoretical and if realized, can understand the thoughts and emotions of other entities thus reflecting how the AI interacts with those around them. In theory, this would allow AI to simulate human-like relationships. Because Theory of Mind AI could infer human motives and reasoning, it would personalize its interactions with individuals based on their unique emotional needs and intentions. Theory of Mind AI probably would also be able to understand and contextualize artwork and essays, which today's generative AI tools are unable to do.

Self-Aware AI

Self-Aware AI can be mapped to upper AI. Like "Theory of Mind AI" this form of AI is strictly theoretical. Once achieved, it might have the ability to understand its own internal conditions and traits along with human emotions and thoughts. It would also have its own set of emotions, needs and beliefs.

As described above, AI System categorization based on functionality or capability demands unique AI techniques. Be it simple tasks, automated, repetitive/mundane tasks or solving complex business problems, AI offers a mix of techniques, as described below.

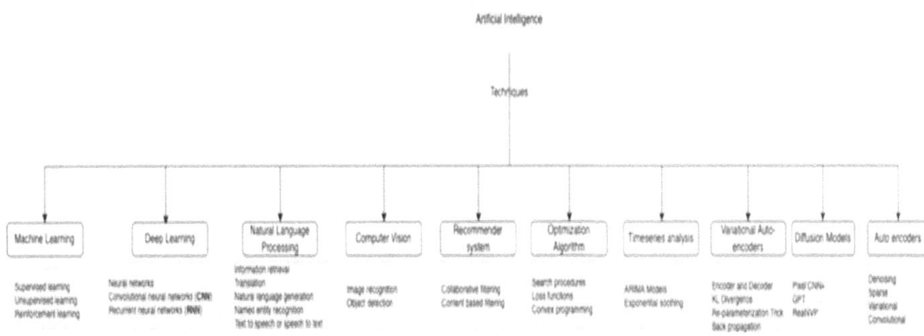

Figure 1.3: Overview of AI Techniques

Machine Learning

Machine learning, at times called **ML,** can be described as a system that learns patterns from the data ingested in it and tries to solve similar problems.

Types of machine learning techniques used extensively are:

- ***Supervised Learning***: A technique that uses labeled datasets to train algorithms to predict outcomes and recognize patterns. This is mostly used for predictive tasks, such as sales forecasting.
- ***Unsupervised Learning***: A technique that discovers hidden patterns from unlabeled data without any explicit instructions. Customer segmentation is an example where unsupervised learning can be applied.
- ***Reinforcement Learning***: A technique used by a Machine Learning system to make decisions to achieve the most optimal results similar to the trial-and-error process that humans use till they achieve desired result. Dynamic pricing or resource allocation are examples where reinforcement learning can be applied.

Deep Learning: Deep learning, the most coveted aspect of AI, is an advanced technique that uses processes like the human brain to solve a given problem. There are many deep learning techniques. Standard techniques used by deep learning are:

- ***Neural Networks***: A technique consisting of elements called interconnected nodes which are known as neurons, organized in layers that function like the human brain. Information is processed through these layers, with each neuron receiving inputs, applying a mathematical operation to them and producing an output. Many complex tasks such as fraud detection and speech recognition benefit from neural network based deep learning techniques.
- ***Convolutional Neural Networks (CNNs)***: A technique consisting of elements called convolutional layers, Pooling layer and fully connected (FC) layers that provide a scalable approach to solving complex tasks such as image and video analysis.

- *Recurrent Neural Networks (RNNs)*: RNNs are deep neural networks trained on sequential or time series data to create a machine learning model supporting sequential predictions or conclusions based on sequential inputs such as demand prediction or stock price analysis.

Natural Language Processing (NLP): Natural language processing, otherwise called NLP, is an approach towards understanding human languages through a machine like a human being. As the name suggests, it uses computational linguistic techniques that focus on understanding, analyzing and interpreting human language in a meaningful and useful way. Some techniques used by NLP are:

- *Information Retrieval:* These are the techniques that identify specific information and its relationship or context in the text.
- *Translation: These* techniques are used to translate text from one language to another, or one form to another.
- *Natural Language Generation: These* techniques are used for generating text that could be an abstract of the content or another representation of the content.
- *Named Entity Recognition:* These techniques are used to identify and classify entities such as people, organization, location etc. in text.
- *Text-to-speech or Speech-to-text conversion:* These techniques are used to convert spoken languages to text and vice-versa.

Computer Vision

As the name suggests, computer vision uses techniques to identify and understand objects or people in images or videos. Techniques used by computer vision are:

- *Image Recognition*: To identify an object or a feature in an image or video. For example, this technique can be used to identify defects in products or automate visual inspections.
- *Facial Recognition*: Like image recognition, this technique helps identify and confirm faces. It is mostly used for enhancing security and customer experience in retail, banking and hospitality industries.
- *Object Detection*: To identify or detect different objects, for example, identifying obstacles during traffic management or in tracking solutions.

Recommender System

A recommender system, as the name suggests, is used to recommend something. For example, it can filter and recommend the right content based on the user's preferences, viewing history etc. Some techniques used by recommender systems are:

- *Collaborative Filtering*: Used to recommend products or content based on user behavior and preferences. It is mostly used in e-commerce applications such as Amazon or streaming services such as Netflix.
- *Content-Based Filtering*: Used to recommend items like those a user has

previously interacted with, using item attributes. This technique is also widely used on e-commerce applications and streaming services.

Optimization Algorithm

In general, an algorithm is defined as a structured approach or process or set of rules that needs to be followed in calculations or problem-solving operations, especially by a computer. As the name suggests, optimization algorithms focus on an optimized approach to solve a business problem. For example, this may refer to a set of algorithms that can help find the best solution to a specific problem such as linear programming for resource allocation or genetic algorithms for route planning. Techniques widely used by optimization algorithms are:

- ***Search procedures:*** To identify optimal value of a function by searching through all possible solutions until one with the highest objective function value is found. It is used mostly for finding information in large data structures.
- ***Loss functions:*** A mathematical technique that quantifies the error margin between a model's prediction and the actual target value.
- ***Convex Programming:*** A technique is used to solve nonlinear equations by considering both equality and inequality constraints simultaneously.

Time series analysis

Time series analysis focuses on analyzing a sequence of data points collected over an interval of time for a specific period. Popular models used in the time series analysis are:

- *ARIMA (autoregressive integrated moving average)* ***Models***: A statistical analysis model, that uses time series data to either understand the data set in a better way or to predict future trends. It is mostly used for demand forecasting, stock price prediction etc. For example, a retail company like Pepsi might use this model to forecast the demand during the holiday season.
- ***Exponential Smoothing***: A time series forecasting method that adapts to changing trends in the data by not focusing on the past observations but by assigning more weight to recent observations. It finds its applicability in problems like inventory management. For example, a corporation might use this to plan for a water crisis in the summer season.

Variational Auto-encoders

Variational auto-encoders (VAE) are AI algorithms used in the context of Generative AI to create new data by using variations of input data that the models are trained on. VAEs use deep learning for generation of new data, anomalies detection and noise removal. They are part of the families of probabilistic graphical models and variational Bayesian methods. Probabilistic graphical models are models that use a graph to represent the conditional dependencies between random variables and are used in fields like statistics, probability theory and machine learning. At the same time variational Bayesian methods provide an analytical approximation to the posterior probability of the unobserved variables, in order to do statistical inference over these variables. Various techniques used in the case of VAEs are:

- *Encoder and decoder:* An encoder is used to transfer a molecular structure into a continuous latent vector and a decoder is used to convert the latent vector back to the molecule in a VAE algorithm.
- *KL divergence:* To measure the difference between two probability distributions.
- *Reparameterization trick:* The reparameterization trick injects randomness while maintaining the relationship between the mean and standard deviation.
- *Backpropagation:* The new equation in the reparameterization trick only involves deterministic operations, which allows the network to learn and adjust its parameters effectively.

Diffusion Models

A diffusion model is a type of generative machine-learning model that transforms random noise into realistic data by iteratively refining it. Its typical implementations include:

- *PixelCNN++:* A generative model mostly used for image generation. It uses autoregressive connections to model images pixel by pixel, decomposing the joint image distribution as a product of conditionals.
- *GPT:* Generative Pre-trained Transformer or GPT is a multimodal large language model released with different versions and created by Open AI. It is widely used for text generation.
- *Real NVP:* A generative model that utilizes real-valued non-volume preserving (real NVP) transformations for density estimation. The model can perform efficient and exact inference, sampling and log-density estimation of data points.

Autoencoders

Autoencoders are a specialized class of AI algorithms designed for unsupervised learning. It can learn efficient representations of input data with no need for labels. Various types of autoencoders are

- *Denoising Autoencoder:* Denoising autoencoders can work on a partially corrupted input. These are neural network models that remove noise from corrupted or noisy data by learning to reconstruct the original data from the noisy version. Hence, it can be trained to recover the original undistorted image from a partially corrupt image. It is an effective way to constrain the network from simply copying the input and thus learn the underlying structure and important features of the data.
- *Sparse Autoencoder:* Sparse autoencoders contain more hidden units than the input but only a few are allowed to be active at once. This property is called

the sparsity of the network. The sparsity of the network can be controlled by either manually zeroing the required hidden units, turning the activation functions or by adding a loss term to the cost function.

- *Variational Autoencoder:* **Variational** autoencoder makes strong assumptions about the distribution of latent variables and uses the Stochastic Gradient Variational Bayes estimator in the training process. It assumes that the data is generated by a Directed Graphical Model and tries to learn an approximation to the conditional property by providing a probabilistic manner for describing an observation in latent space. Thus, rather than building an encoder that gives an output of a single value to describe each latent state attribute, a probability distribution for each latent attribute is provided.
- *Convolutional Autoencoder:* Convolutional autoencoders are a type of autoencoder that use convolutional neural networks (CNNs) as their building blocks. The encoder consists of multiple layers that take an image or a grid as input and pass it through different convolution layers thus forming a compressed representation of the input. The decoder is the mirror image of the encoder. It deconvolves the compressed representation and tries to reconstruct the original image.The techniques described above are critical based on the type of AI application. These techniques also demonstrate the technical complexity that AI applications may have to address business problems. The evolution of these techniques has taken many years. Some of the key milestones during the evolution of AI is further explained below.

Key milestones in AI development

Though AI is known for its technical revolution in the last ten-twenty years, the concepts of AI were founded in the early 1940s. The technology has survived multiple ups and downs especially, two major winters in 1974 - 1980 and 1987 - 2000 before industry accepted the true value of AI.A few key milestones in the evolution of AI in chronological order are captured below.

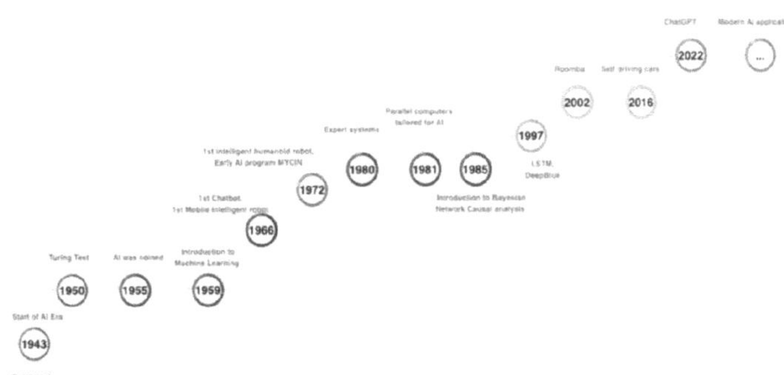

Figure 1.4: Evolution of AI

The first model of artificial neurons, which is now recognized as the first work done on AI was proposed by Warren McCulloch and Walter pits in **1943**. This started the era of AI. In **1950**, the English mathematician Alan Turing published "**Computing Machinery and Intelligence**" in which he proposed a test that can check the machine's ability to exhibit intelligent behavior equivalent to human intelligence, known as **Turing test.** This gave birth to the concept of AI. In **1951,** the initial artificial neural network (ANN) named Stochastic Neural Analog Reinforcement Calculator (SNARC) was built by Marvin Minsky and Dean Edmonds, supported by John von Neumann. This utilized 3,000 vacuum tubes to mimic a network of 40 neurons and was designed to learn from experience and improve its performance through a process of trial and error. This was the first AI experiment and was an important milestone in the early development of AI. In **1952**, the world's first self-learning program for playing games "The Samuel Checkers-Playing Program" was pioneered by Arthur Samuel. *Arthur Samuel was the pioneer in machine learning and won the Computer Pioneer Award by IEEE in 1987.* In **1955,** Allen Newell and Herbert A. Simon created the "first artificial intelligence program" named as **"Logic Theorist"**, that proved 38 of 52 Mathematics theorems. In the same year, John McCarthy, then a young Assistant Professor of Mathematics at Dartmouth College, decided to organize a group to clarify and develop ideas about thinking machines. He picked the name **'Artificial Intelligence'** (**AI**) for the new field. In August that year, a document, known as the "Dartmouth proposal", was drawn up by four academicians John McCarthy, Marvin Minsky, Nathaniel Rochester, and Claude Shannon, that examined few key themes in fields of research that included **neural networks, the theory of computability**, **creativity** and **natural language processing** and **recognition.** During the same time, high-level computer languages such as FORTRAN, LISP, or COBOL were invented. In **1958**, one of the early artificial neural networks called perceptrons was introduced by Frank Rosenblatt, which had the ability to learn from data. This invention laid the foundation for **modern neural networks**. Simultaneously, John McCarthy developed the LISP programming language, which was favored by the AI community and became highly popular among the developers. In **1959, Arthur** Samuel introduced the phrase "**machine learning**" in a pivotal paper in which he proposed that computers could be programmed to surpass their creators in performance. Additionally, Oliver Selfridge made a notable contribution to machine learning with his publication "**Pandemonium: A Paradigm for Learning**". This work outlined a model capable of self-improvement, enabling it to discover patterns in events more effectively.

In **1964,** Daniel Borrow, a doctoral candidate at MIT, created STUDENT, one of the **early programs** for **natural language processing (NLP)**, for solving algebra word problems. In **1966**, Joseph Weizenbaum created the **first chatbot**, which was named ELIZA. Furthermore, Stanford Research Institute created **Shakey**, the earliest **mobile intelligent robot** incorporating AI, computer vision, navigation and NLP, which can be considered a precursor to today's self-driving cars and drones. In **1969,** Arthur Bryson and Yu-Chi Ho outlined a learning algorithm known as **back propagation**, which enabled the development of multilayer artificial neural networks. This also laid the groundwork for deep learning. Additionally, Marvin Minsky and Seymour Papert authored the book "Perceptron's," which elucidated the **constraints of basic neural networks**. This publication led to a decline in neural network research and a resurgence in symbolic AI research. In **1972**, the first intelligent humanoid robot was built in Japan, which was named WABOT-1. In the same year, MYCIN, an early AI program that helped physicians in diagnosing and treating bacterial infections, was developed by Stanford university. It was an interactive program and could answer simple English questions and explain its knowledge of infectious disease therapy. At the same time, experts could also teach MYCIN therapeutic decision rules. The first national conference of the American Association of Artificial Intelligence was held at Stanford University in **1980**. The same year expert systems were programmed to emulate the decision-making ability of a human expert. In **1981**, Parallel computers tailored for AI and various computational functions were created by Danny Hillis. This featured architecture akin to contemporary GPUs. Another important concept called Bayesian network causal analysis was introduced by Judea Pearl for encoding uncertainty in computer systems in **1985**. This was a statistical method for understanding the relationships between variables and making probabilistic inferences about cause and effect. This is currently applied in multiple modern AI techniques, especially ones involving decision making and natural language processing.

1997 was historical as IBM's Deep Blue, a chess playing expert system which runs on a unique purpose-built IBM supercomputer achieved a historic milestone by defeating world chess champion Gary Kasparov, marking the first ever computer victory over a reigning world chess champion. Around the same time, Sepp Hochreiter and Jürgen Schmidhuber introduced the Long Short-Term Memory recurrent neural network (**LSTM**), revolutionizing the capability to process entire sequences of data such as speech or video. In **2002**, for the first time, AI entered homes in the form of Roomba, a vacuum cleaner by a company named iRobot. **2006** saw a new change when organizations like Facebook, Twitter, Netflix started using AI. Slowly, major advancements in AI with a mix of techniques such as deep learning, Big Data and related technical innovations triggered the growth that we see today in AI. The generation alpha was lucky to experience the modern AI systems in the form of games, social media experience, internet of things (IOT) devices and so on. In **2011** Jürgen Schmidhuber, Dan Claudiu Cirean, Ueli Meier and Jonathan Masci created the initial Convolutional Neural Network (**CNN**) model that attained "superhuman" performance by emerging as the winner in the "German Traffic Sign Recognition" competition. At the same time, Siri, a voice-activated personal assistant, capable of generating responses and executing actions in response to voice commands was launched by Apple. IBM's Watson won Jeopardy, a quiz shows where it solved complex questions as well as riddles, proving its capability to understand and process natural languages. In **2012**, Google launched an Android app feature, "Google Now", which was able to provide information to the user as a prediction, based on deep learning technology. Further, Geoffrey Hinton, Ilya Sutskever and Alex Krizhevsky presented a deep convolutional neural network (CNN) structure that emerged victorious in the ImageNet challenge. Imagenet challenge focused on evaluation of algorithms for object detection and image classification. This achievement further sparked proliferation of research and application in the field of deep learning. In **2013**, China's Tianhe-2 system achieved a remarkable feat by doubling the speed of the world's leading supercomputers to reach 33.86 petaflops.

Furthermore, DeepMind unveiled deep reinforcement learning, a CNN that acquired skills through repetitive learning and rewards, ultimately surpassing human experts in playing games. Also, Google researcher Tomas Mikolov and his team introduced Word2vec, a tool designed to automatically discern the semantic connections among words. Currently Word2vec is used to produce word embeddings and majorly used in natural language processing techniques. In **2014**, chatbot "Eugene Goostman" won a competition in the infamous "Turing test." Whereas Ian Goodfellow and his team pioneered generative adversarial networks (GANs), a type of machine learning framework employed for producing images, altering pictures, and crafting deepfakes. Diederik Kingma and Max Welling introduced variational autoencoders (VAEs) for generating images, videos, and text. Also, Facebook engineered the DeepFace deep learning facial recognition system to identify human faces in digital images with accuracy nearly comparable to human capabilities.

There are so many demonstrations of AI capabilities that can help in real life after that. For example, in **2016**, Uber initiated a pilot program for self-driving cars in Pittsburgh, catering to a limited group of users. In **2018,** the "Project Debater" from IBM debated on complex topics with two master debaters and performed extremely well. In **2021**, OpenAI unveiled the Dall-E multimodal AI system, capable of producing images based on textual prompts. In **2022**, OpenAI launched ChatGPT, offering a chat-oriented interface to its GPT-3.5 LLM. The latest being in **2024**, Wimbeldon Tennis was powered by IBM Watson X, an enterprise-ready generative AI platform from IBM that used AI to provide an experience while viewing a Tennis match.

The key milestones in AI development also are a demonstration of the power that AI techniques have and how it influences modern applications. The next section discusses how AI is adopted in modern applications.

AI in modern applications

The story of modern applications can be attributed to the current era also called the contemporary era or the Information Age. It is characterized by developments in technology that have changed the way humans work. Through the invention of computers and other smart devices, access to information has become much easier and faster, helping in better human interaction and connection. Based on demands of the information age, specialized applications focusing on advanced technologies such as BigData, analytics, cloud, mobile, internet etc can be called modern applications. As evident from the above sections, one of the big roles in transforming modern applications is played by AI. The technical evolution of AI in the last ten years has changed the ways industries operate. AI-driven automation benefits many industries by optimizing various business processes such as regulatory compliance, customer service and bringing in innovative digital solutions. For example, in banking, AI is used to streamline complex banking processes by leveraging technologies like optical character recognition (OCR) and voice-activated programs to enhance efficiency and accuracy. AI technologies streamlined tasks such as document scanning, data extraction and customer

information retrieval, enabling organizations to allocate resources strategically and maximize productivity. Chatbots for customer service is another area where many industries or organizations benefit by enhancing customer service experience through instant responses to queries, personalized advice, reduced response time, to name a few. Overall, the transformation for each industry is unique.
A few examples of the modern application of AI are captured below.

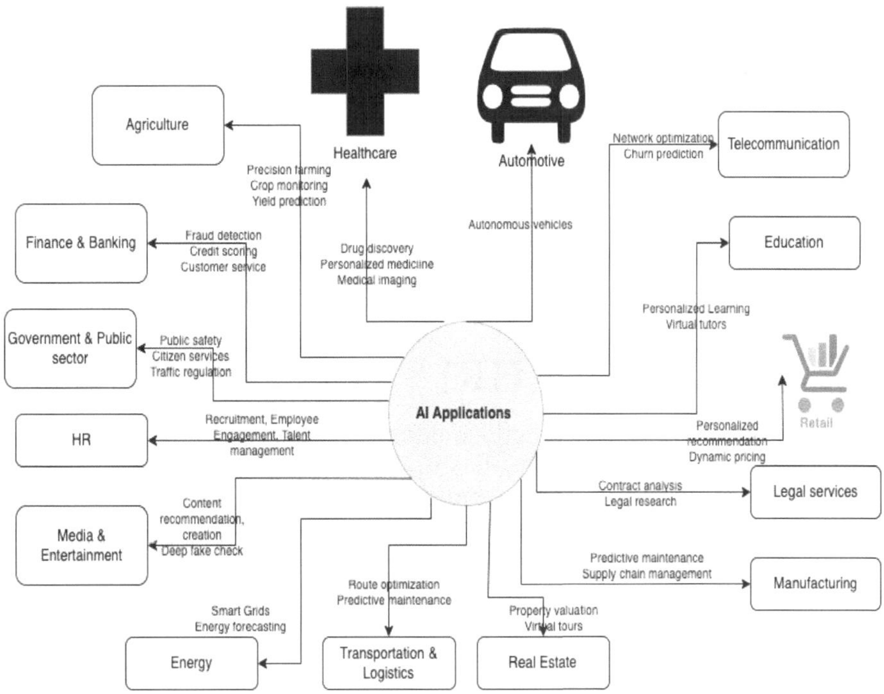

Figure 1.5: Application of AI in various industries

Agriculture Industry

Many government organizations and farmers are leveraging AI for precision farming to analyze data from sensors, drones and satellites to optimize planting, watering, harvesting or improving crop quality. Predicting quality of crop and crop yield based on multiple parameters such as environmental conditions, soil quality, historical data and additional parameters as appropriate cannot be achieved through manual analysis.

Finance & Banking industry

Apart from reporting and compliance needs, many banks leverage AI for real-time fraud detection and prevention by analysing transaction patterns, identifying anomalies and flagging potentially fraudulent activities. Another area, where many banks have transformed their business is through credit scoring and risk assessment of individuals and businesses, leading to more effective risk management, empowering financial institutions to make well-informed lending decisions. Anti-Money Laundering (AML) compliance is another area where AI is leveraged to analyse vast amounts of transaction data detecting suspicious patterns and identifying potential money laundering activities, helping financial institutions comply with regulatory requirements and mitigate risks.

Government & Public sector

Government industries or organizations innovatively use AI to analyze crime data to predict and prevent criminal activities thus enhancing public safety. Many countries use AI to improve citizen services, traffic management, crowd management, infrastructure planning and development etc.

Human Resources (HR)

HR is an industry which has mostly manual driven for a long time. However, with the advent of AI, this industry has undergone a major change in the way it operates. For example, using AI for candidate assessment and job role fitment has improved the recruitment process. Similarly, monitoring employee satisfaction and engagement or analyzing 360-degree employee information has significantly improved employee engagement or talent management experience.

Media & Entertainment

Platforms such as Netflix or Spotify powered with AI dominate almost every household as part of entertainment. These platforms employ AI algorithms to analyze user behavior, creating personalized playlists for an enhanced entertainment discovery experience. AI elevates game design by improving non-player characters and refining mechanics, creating realistic and challenging levels that enhance the player's experience. New content creation, content generation, content enhancement using AI techniques have helped authors/creators create more captivating narratives and a mesmerizing experience for the viewer. AI-powered recommendation engines analyze diverse user data to predict and promote relevant content, enhancing user engagement and satisfaction. Platforms like Netflix leverage machine learning to continuously improve content recommendations based on A/B testing and user interactions.

Energy

In the energy industry, AI has multiple applications, including optimizing the distribution and consumption of electricity, balancing supply and demand in real-time such as smart grid, predictive maintenance for monitoring energy infrastructure to predict failures in power plants, grids and pipeline, forecasting availability of energy sources.

Transportation and Logistics

AI empowers travel/transportation/logistics companies to create personalized itineraries based on individual preferences and provide real time travel updates and recommendations. AI algorithms are used to determine the most efficient or optimized routes reducing fuel consumption and time to destination, predictive maintenance of vehicles and many more.

Real Estate

AI models assess the value of real estate properties based on factors like location, market trends and amenities. In many cases, it provides virtual reality (VR) based solutions that allow potential buyers to tour properties remotely improving buyer experience.

Manufacturing

AI can help monitor equipment health to predict failures before they occur, reducing downtime and maintenance costs; optimizes production schedules, manages inventory and predicts supply chain bottlenecks.

Legal services

AI can help analyze legal documents for relevant information, speeding up the review process; assist lawyers in finding relevant case law, statutes and legal precedents or automatically review and flag issues in contracts, reducing the risk of legal disputes.

Telecommunication

With the advancement in technologies such as 5G/6G in the telecom industry, AI is used to optimize network performance, reduce latency and improve service quality, prevent fraud or even predict customer churn to roll out retention plans.

Automotive

AI has transformed the automotive industry through self-driving cars, trucks and drones, enhancing safety and efficiency.

Healthcare

Some of the lifesaving advancements happening in healthcare can be attributed to AI. For example, AI can be used to diagnose diseases from medical images like X-rays, MRIs and CT scans. AI can further help accelerate discovery and development of new drugs by predicting interaction of different compounds with targets in the human body, creating personalized treatment plans for improving outcomes and reducing side effects.

Education

Education industry has seen multiple new approaches to the existing system due to the use of AI. Some of them include personalized learning, where AI is used to tailor educational content to individual student needs, improving learning outcomes, or engaging with virtual tutors to provide additional help to students.

Retail

Apart from using AI for personalized recommendations, retail organizations use AI for inventory management, where AI predicts demand for products, optimizes stock levels or dynamic pricing to adjust prices in real-time based on factors like customer behavior, competition to name a few. The above list describes only a few examples of the use of AI in the modern world. There are far more uses and many other industries like consumer products benefit immensely through the adoption of AI. With wider application of AI across industries it is important to adopt security, ethics and governance for AI based applications to prevent misuse of technology and ensure safety for mankind.

Conclusion

This chapter is an introductory chapter that briefly describes the evolution of AI, techniques used in AI and its potential application in various industries. While AI applications are critical for the success of each industry, it is also important to understand that technology is used in an ethical way and the systems can be trusted blindly to exploit its full capability. In the next chapter, we will focus on understanding the ethical challenges and considerations for AI application development and deployment.

Chapter 2

The Ethical Implications of AI

In **Chapter 1**, we introduced Artificial Intelligence (**AI**), exploring its advancements and how it is utilized across various industries. We learned how AI can simplify existing tasks and make them more efficient. Overall, AI is a powerful tool that significantly benefits individuals and society. It supports, complements, and empowers people in diverse work and daily life areas.

Now, let us delve into the concept of ethics. Ethics refers to moral principles and rules that guide us in distinguishing between right and wrong. AI ethics is a domain focused on maximizing the benefits and value of AI while minimizing its risks and potential harm to individuals and society. It emphasizes innovation with responsibility.

If we analyze the responsibilities of AI ethics, they can be divided among the various personas involved in developing AI systems.

1. Designers and developers are responsible for creating systems that are impartial, transparent, accountable, and respectful of individual privacy.
2. Industries and organizations must prioritize key aspects such as leveraging AI for positive purposes, maintaining transparency, understanding its impact, and establishing ethical governance boards and frameworks.
3. Governments and regulatory bodies work to establish regulations and laws that ensure fairness, safety, and accountability. They mandate oversight and auditing, promote inclusion by equitably distributing benefits, and aim to reduce disparities. Additionally, they address global AI challenges through international collaborations.

AI ethics is essential for building trustworthy AI systems that benefit society and prevent harm. A comprehensive framework is necessary to ensure AI acts as a force for good, with shared responsibility among all stakeholders to mitigate potential risks.
In recent years, significant investments by OpenAI and other technology partners have driven substantial advancements in AI, leading to its rapid adoption in businesses and everyday consumer interactions.

In this chapter, we will cover the following topics:

* AI Ethical Considerations or Challenges
* Ethical principles and frameworks that can help in addressing these challenges

AI Ethical Considerations or Challenges

As Artificial intelligence (AI) continues to grow and advance, it is also being adopted across various sectors of society. Ethical considerations in its development and deployment have become the topmost concerns for organizations while adopting AI. Let us try to understand these ethical challenges. I will explain the ethical challenges of AI. Below (**Fig.2.1**) are the topmost ethical challenges with AI projects.

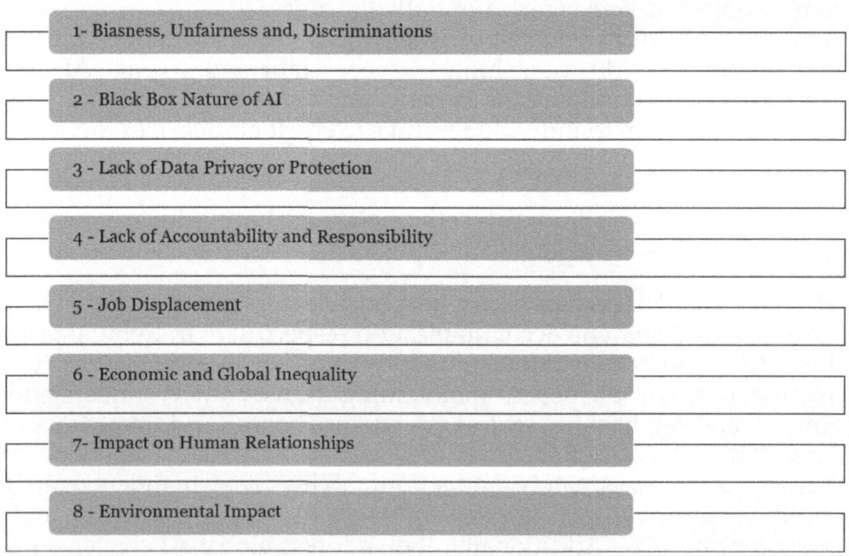

Figure 2.1: AI Ethical Challenges

Biasness, Unfairness, and Discriminations

Biasness, Unfairness, and Discrimination refer to system outcomes in which certain people or groups do not get the same benefits or opportunities due to biased AI predictions or decisions.

These concerns can arise from multiple sources, including:

a. Training Data: AI models learn or train from historical data, which may reflect existing social prejudices. The example below concerns training data that leads to biased or unfair outcomes.
b. Algorithm Design: Developers may unknowingly embed biases into algorithms when they structure decision-making rules.
For example - The data used to train the models, the algorithms' design and the way AI is implemented in practical situations are some of the possible origins of this bias. It can manifest in many ways, including social and economic factors and racial or gender biases, and it can have terrible consequences. This can lead to biased outcomes like loan/mortgage approval, law enforcement, etc.

Figure 2.2: Source of AI biases

Please find some real-world examples on this subject

Facial Recognition Systems:

Police departments use this facial recognition system for surveillance. Such facial recognition technologies perform poorly on individuals with darker skin tones and women's faces. This system could wrongly identify people of color, which could lead to their exposure to unlawful arrests and discrimination. The reason behind this system's unbiased and unfair result is the training datasets. These datasets were heavily twisted toward lighter-skinned faces, causing the system to be less accurate in recognizing or identifying darker-skinned people or underrepresented groups in the datasets.

Hiring Algorithm:

Amazon automated an internal hiring tool that leveraged AI. This tool was built using an algorithm that could review resumes and determine which applicants Amazon should bring on board. This AI-powered hiring tool was identified as biased against female applicants. This tool preferred male candidates over equally qualified female applicants for technical jobs. This AI system used an algorithm based on past hiring practices that favored men, embedding historical biases into the decision-making logic.

Predictive Policing:

Predictive policing AI algorithms or Tools used to forecast criminal activity in the U.S. The tools identify hot spots, and the police plan to patrol around these tip-offs. There was a parallel tool to predict criminal who has a high chance of being involved in future criminal activity. In this tool, bias caused by algorithm choices is the case of the COMPAS algorithm. This example highlights how algorithm design choices can introduce bias, such as which features to emphasize and how outcomes are weighed. These algorithms' designs focus on historical crime data, criminal age, gender, marital status, history of substance abuse, address, zip code, etc.

Given that AI's role is critical in such a use case, these systems must make more equitable decisions based on human judgment or ad hoc rules. If left unchecked, bias in AI can have profound social and economic consequences.

Black Box Nature of AI - Transparency and Explainability Implications

The main challenge is how to prevent harm caused by algorithmic decisions. As AI becomes more dominant in society and individual lives, the issues of expandability and traceability (tracking how decisions are made) become more critical.

A key concern is the "opacity" (lack of clarity) in AI systems making decisions. This is often called the "black box" problem, where it is difficult to understand how machine learning algorithms process inputs and make predictions.

Sometimes, AI developers and engineers are also not fully clear on how these AI models or systems arrive at a specific outcome based on provided input. This lack of expandability and transparency is often called AI's "black box" problem.

When AI systems are not transparent, and their decisions are hard to explain, they raise serious ethical concerns. Explaining how a system arrives at its outcomes or decisions is essential; otherwise, it becomes difficult to trust it. Such challenges arise due to factors.

Complexity of AI Model Architecture & Algorithms:

Modern AI models, such as neural networks or deep learning systems, operate with thousands or millions of sophisticated parameters and massive layers of computations, making them difficult to understand, explain, and interpret. These challenges for explainability arise due to the following reasons:

High Dimensionality and Millions of Parameters

Neural networks have layers of interconnected neurons, with each connection associated with a weight (parameter). As models grow deeper (more layers) and broader (more neurons), they can contain millions or billions of parameters.
For Example, GPT-based language models have over 175 billion parameters. It becomes impossible for developers to manually track how each parameter contributes to the final decision or output.

Non-Linear Relationships and Feature Interactions:

AI models, especially deep learning networks, capture non-linear patterns and interactions between input features that are not easily visible or interpretable. For instance, in a healthcare model, the interaction between multiple lab results, lifestyle habits, and genetic data may predict disease risks—but it's hard to pinpoint which features played the most critical role.
Impact: Unlike simpler models (like linear regression), these complex patterns make it difficult to explain the reasoning behind predictions.

Black-Box Nature of Learning Process

AI models, such as convolutional neural networks (CNNs) for image recognition or transformers for natural language processing, learn patterns through multiple layers of transformation. However, the intermediate steps (like how specific neurons get activated) are not always interpretable to humans.
Impact: Even developers cannot easily explain why the model chose one decision over another because it is hidden within layers of transformations.

Sensitivity to Data and Hyperparameters

AI models are highly sensitive to the quality and quantity of data they are trained on. Minor changes in training data or hyperparameter settings (like learning rate or number of epochs) can lead to significantly different outputs.
Impact: This makes it hard to trace how small changes affect the model's behavior, leading to challenges in debugging and ensuring consistency.

* **Use of Proprietary Models and Trade Secrets** - Many companies keep their AI algorithms confidential to protect their intellectual property and competitive advantage. This secrecy limits transparency, as external reviewers or users cannot fully understand or audit how the system works.
* **Insufficient Documentation** – Sometimes, AI systems are developed quickly, and the underlying decisions (like data selection or model choices) may not be well-documented. Tracing how and why the AI makes specific decisions becomes difficult without proper documentation.

Please find a few real-world examples of such concerns in AI Applications.
Healthcare: Watson for Oncology: The AI oncology solution was created to assist medical professionals in treating cancer patients. However, doctors found it difficult to understand how the system arrived at its suggestions. The AI would make beneficial suggestions without offering a comprehensive justification for its judgments. Doctors found it challenging to trust the AI's recommendations because of this lack of transparency and explainability, particularly when such advice conflicts with established medical practices.

Financial Credit Scoring: Financial firms widely use AI models to evaluate loan applications and compute credit scores. These models analyze large volumes of data, such as past payments, spending patterns, and other financial activities. However, the algorithms are frequently so complex that even the creators find it difficult to justify a given action, like rejecting a loan application or providing a specific interest rate. This opacity can lead to frustration among consumers who cannot understand why they were deemed a credit risk.

Lack of Data Privacy or Protection

AI systems need large amounts of data for training and predictions, which creates privacy and security concerns. Collecting, storing, and using personal information – like health records, financial details, or online behavior – can lead to serious risks such as data misuse, data breaches, or invasion of privacy. These risks are especially serious, where personal data plays a key role in AI decisions.

Let's understand how these challenges are infused

Massive Data Collection and Surveillance Risks

AI systems often require large amounts of data, which raises concerns about surveillance (such as tracking user activities) and misuse of personal information.

For Example, Location-based apps that use AI to suggest services but unintentionally reveal users' personal movements.

Risk of Data Breaches and Cyberattacks

AI systems often store sensitive data in centralized repositories. If this data is hacked, it could result in financial loss and reputational damage.

Inference and Re-identification Risks

AI algorithms can infer sensitive information about individuals, even from anonymized or de-identified data (without names, addresses, or personal identifiers). This happens because AI can detect patterns and correlations in the data, which might allow it to infer an individual's identity or predict medical conditions.
Example: An AI model trained on health data predicting a person's medical condition with high probability. Please find some real-world use cases.

Corporate Surveillance: Corporate surveillance refers to the monitoring, collection, and analysis of employee or customer data by companies to optimize operations, improve marketing, or manage workforce productivity. However, this practice raises significant data privacy and protection challenges, as it can invade personal privacy and be misused.

* **Invasion of Privacy:** Employees may feel their personal space is violated, especially if the monitoring continues beyond working hours (e.g., tracking laptop activity late at night).
* **Data Security Risks:** The collected data may include sensitive personal information, such as private messages or browsing history. If Company X's security systems are compromised or the data is not stored properly, it could lead to data breaches, exposing employees' personal data to hackers.
* **Consent and Transparency Issues:** Employees may not be fully aware of what data is being collected, how it is used, or how long it is retained. Workers could feel compelled to accept unpleasant monitoring without clear policies and consent mechanisms.
* **Legal and Regulatory Violations:** Many jurisdictions have strict privacy regulations, such as GDPR (in Europe) or CCPA (in California). If Company X collects excessive data without employee consent, it could violate these laws and face penalties

Smart Cities: Public Surveillance with Facial Recognition: Cities like London and Shenzhen use facial recognition in CCTV networks to monitor traffic, detect crimes, and manage crowds. There are several Privacy and Protection Challenges:

* **Mass Surveillance**: Continuous monitoring of public spaces can interfere with citizens' privacy rights.

* **Data Breaches**: If public databases storing biometric data are hacked, sensitive information could be exposed.

Lack of Accountability and Responsibility

As AI systems become more autonomous, it becomes increasingly difficult to determine who is accountable when things go wrong – the developers, companies, end-users, or the AI system itself. As human oversight becomes less significant, incidents caused by AI can lead to legal, ethical, and operational challenges concerning accountability. Establishing precise rules and frameworks for allocating accountability is essential to promoting trust and fairness in applying AI technologies. Below are examples illustrating these challenges.

Autonomous Cars: In 2018, an Uber self-driving car struck and killed a pedestrian in Arizona. The AI system misinterpreted the pedestrian as a human being and did not react appropriately to stop the collision.
Multiple stakeholders were involved in this system, including 1) Uber, which deployed the AI system; 2) Engineers responsible for the AI's development; and 3) A backup safety driver, whose role was to intervene if the system failed. Who will be accountable for errors when things go wrong in this AI System?

* Who is responsible? Should Uber be held accountable for this incident as they deployed and operated the AI system, or should the engineers who built the AI system be held responsible?
* Role of human oversight: Was the backup driver careless, or did the system fail too quickly for them to respond?

It was challenging to decide who should be held accountable for the deadly accident due to unclear accountability and responsibility. The lack of clear guidelines on the division of responsibilities between human drivers and AI makes it difficult to assign legal liability. **AI Algorithm in Finance Trading:** AI algorithms are widely used in the financial markets to execute trades at high speeds. Sometimes, algorithms have made erroneous trades, triggering market volatility or even market crashes. For example, the 2010 Flash Crash saw the U.S. stock market lose nearly $1 trillion in minutes due to automated trading algorithms. Who will be accountable for errors when things go wrong in this AI System?

* **System error or human oversight?** When trades lead to unintended consequences, is the issue due to flawed algorithms or insufficient human monitoring of the system?
* **Algorithmic black box:** Many AI trading algorithms operate as black boxes, making it difficult to trace the origin of the error or identify which specific decision caused market disruption.
* **The financial industry involves multiple parties** – developers, traders, and regulatory bodies. Determining whether the fault lies with AI algorithm

design, deployment, or improper use is complex.

Key Challenges in AI Accountability

* **Multiple Stakeholders Involved:** When AI acts autonomously, it becomes difficult to determine where **liability starts and ends.** Accountability and responsibility must be divided between developers, companies, end-users, and regulators.
* **Complex AI Systems (Black Box Problem)**: Many AI models are not fully explainable, which limits the ability to trace the cause of an error. Opaque decision-making complicates efforts to assign responsibility.
* **Reduced Human Supervision**: AI systems often operate independently, making it hard to determine whether human intervention is needed. If responsibility is unclear, accountability gaps emerge.
* **Legal and Ethical Uncertainty**: Legal systems may need new frameworks to address shared responsibility among AI systems and humans. Sometimes, current regulations struggle to keep pace with AI developments, which leads to grey areas in liability laws.

Job Displacement: Artificial Intelligence (AI) is rapidly transforming our way of life and work. AI is revolutionizing industries by automating monotonous jobs and optimizing procedures, which boosts output and raises the possibility of job displacement. Employees in these industries risk losing their employment when AI systems take over these responsibilities. Organizations are ethically obligated to assist impacted workers through reskilling and transition programs, even as AI creates new opportunities and doors with new roles and responsibilities.

Let's look at a few real-world examples

Tesla's Gigafactories and AI-Driven Manufacturing

Tesla has become a prominent example of integrating AI-driven technologies in car assembly. Its Gigafactories, located worldwide (in the U.S., China, Germany, and beyond), use cutting-edge automation and artificial intelligence to streamline the production of electric vehicles (EVs). Tesla employs robotic arms for welding, assembling, painting, and material handling. Advanced robots handle repetitive and complex manufacturing processes, such as battery pack assembly. AI-powered systems monitor machinery and predict when equipment might fail or need servicing, reducing downtime and costly disruptions.

Please refer below to the implications on Jobs and Operations at Tesla:

* **Job Displacement and Creation**: Tesla reduced some manual assembly jobs and created new jobs for robotic engineers, AI specialists, and maintenance technicians. Tesla ensures skilling and training workers in operating and

maintaining automated systems.

Increased Production Efficiency: Tesla's Gigafactories achieved higher output with reduced errors

Challenges and Solutions: Initially, excessive dependence on automation caused production delays. Tesla admitted that integrating human oversight and intervention is essential to ensure smooth operations alongside automation. Tesla adjusts its workers for tasks like final inspections and fine assembly, where precision is crucial.

Vodafone's AI Chatbot "TOBi"

The rise of AI-driven chatbots in customer support transforms how businesses interact with customers. While chatbots offer 24/7 availability, faster response times, and cost-efficiency, they also pose a job displacement challenge for human customer service representatives.

Vodafone introduced TOBi, an AI-powered chatbot, to handle billing inquiries, account management, and troubleshooting.

TOBi was able to manage 70% of customer inquiries, significantly reducing the workload on human agents.

Human agents were retrained to focus on more complex customer interactions, such as conflict resolution and service recovery, ensuring minimal job losses.

Impact of AI-Powered Chatbots on Customer Support

Increased Efficiency and Cost Savings - Chatbots can handle **high volumes of inquiries simultaneously**, reducing customer wait times. Automated responses lower the need for large customer service teams, minimizing operational costs.

Improved Customer Experience - AI-driven bots offer personalized interactions by analyzing customer data and providing tailored solutions. Available round-the-clock, they ensure consistent support across different time zones.

Customer Service roles & responsibilities shifts - Chatbots handle routine queries (e.g., FAQs, order status), while complex issues are escalated to human agents. Human agents must increasingly focus on emotional support, conflict resolution, and technical troubleshooting.

Job Displacement: Reduction in Entry-Level Customer Service Jobs. Workers need to be upskilled for roles requiring empathy, creativity, and technical expertise.

Economic & Global Inequality

Recent Artificial Intelligence (AI) developments have significantly boosted productivity and enabled business cost savings. However, these advancements have also widened the wealth gap. The organizations and individuals who own and leverage these technologies benefit greatly, while many workers are displaced as their jobs become automated. These technologies have created high-paying tech professions in bigger / metro cities and created economic inequality in other cities of the country. This trend has resulted in economic inequality within and between countries, with wealth concentrated in regions where AI is developed and deployed at scale.

Please refer to the challenges related to economic and global inequality.

Uneven Distribution of AI Benefits and Global Digital Divide

Global adoption of AI is not consistent. Because of their technological infrastructure, research capacity, and access to trained labor, wealthier nations—including the United States, China, and EU members—benefit most economically. The digital divide is widened because many low-income nations lack the resources—capital, infrastructure, and talent—necessary to develop or apply AI technology.

The digital divide is widened by

AI-powered industries tend to cluster in **wealthy urban centers** or tech hubs, where high-paying jobs are created. In contrast, rural regions and smaller cities in developed and developing countries struggle to attract AI-driven investments, deepening the urban-rural divide.

Countries lagging in AI innovation risk becoming economically marginalized, dependent on wealthier nations for technology and services, and missing out on future economic opportunities. This growing gap contributes to global **geopolitical tensions** and economic instability.

The Role of AI in Market Power and Economic Inequality

Big international corporations use AI to control international marketplaces, frequently displacing smaller competitors. Amazon, for instance, employs AI to optimize price, product recommendations, and logistics, making it very hard for smaller e-commerce companies to compete. As a result, there is a winner-take-all situation in which a few businesses control most of the market value while smaller competitors fight for survival.

AI's Impact on Education and Skills Development

Virtual tutors and AI-powered personalized learning platforms have the potential to revolutionize education, but their advantages are not equally shared. Educational institutions in rich nations or districts have the means to implement these technologies, which will enhance student performance and future employability. However, these resources are unavailable to impoverished schools, especially those in rural areas and low-income nations. Students from these areas consequently lag, restricting social mobility and feeding inequality cycles.

Challenges and the Need for Inclusive AI Development

In addition to widening already-existing economic gaps, unequal access to AI technology jeopardizes international collaboration. As developed economies improve, countries left behind may experience social instability, unemployment, and stagnation. In the absence of a concerted effort to guarantee that the advantages of AI are distributed fairly, the digital divide will keep growing, resulting in an unstable world.

Impact on Human Relationships

As AI technology is progressively incorporated and integrated into our daily lives, many issues that arise from AI's influence on human relationships and decision-making may affect, for example, how individuals connect, engage, and understand social dynamics.

AI Influence on Human Decision-Making

AI-driven recommendation engines and virtual assistants influence our choices in subtle ways. For example, they suggest products on Amazon, meals to order, or shows to watch on TV. These AI systems subtly guide users' choices, often aligning them with pre-defined preferences or trending content, which may limit exposure to new ideas, products, or diverse media.
Example: Platforms like Amazon, Netflix, and food delivery services influence choices by suggesting what to buy, watch, or eat based on user behavior.
Due to such implications, this can shape user habits, preferences, and even beliefs over time, reducing individual agency by pushing decisions that align with an algorithm's suggestions rather than organic curiosity or exploration.

AI Companions Redefining Human Relationships & Connection

AI Companions are redefining human relationships in the Digital Age: Artificial Intelligence (AI) has started to replace humans in positions that were previously limited to friends and partners, etc., in an era when technology is becoming increasingly integrated into every area of our lives. This developing relationship between humans and AI always leads to thinking about the potential consequences of substituting human interaction with digital entities.

Please find real-world examples.

Replika is an example of an AI companion. The purpose of this AI chatbot is to offer emotional assistance. Through text exchanges, users engage with Replika, and over time, the AI learns to offer more tailored responses that replicate a real emotional connection.

Gatebox is another example. They have developed a virtual, life-like AI companion, furthering the concept. With the goal of providing a sense of presence and companionship to individuals who live alone, Gatebox's AI avatar can welcome users home, send messages throughout the day, and even operate smart home appliances.

There are implications as well. Elderly individuals who use AI-powered home assistants or social robots for companionship may become increasingly isolated from human contact. While these technologies can provide some level of interaction, they may also discourage efforts to maintain or build real human relationships. This makes worse feelings of loneliness and social isolation, particularly among vulnerable populations who may already struggle with limited social interactions.

Environmental Impact

The challenge on the environment revolves around the environmental impact of developing, training, and running AI systems, especially large-scale models and data centers While it is helping to create the sustainable solutions for energy intensive industries.

Here are a few real-world use cases where AI Applications were deployed to create sustainable solutions

Use of AI for optimizing logistics in global shipping companies

AI is used by businesses like UPS and Maersk to enhance route planning, optimize fuel usage, and cut down on idle time, all of which can result in considerable fuel savings and lower emissions. However, to interpret real-time data, monitor routes, and adapt to changing conditions like traffic or weather patterns, the AI systems used to evaluate these intricate logistics networks require high energy consumption and resource-intensive hardware. So overall, it brings a dual challenge.

Here are the key challenges involved

High Energy Consumption: Training Large AI Models: The training of advanced AI models, such as language and deep neural networks, require a large amount of processing power and energy.

Data Center Operations: AI models frequently operate on data centers, which have a constant energy requirement due to their ongoing cooling, security, and maintenance needs.

Resource-Intensive Hardware: AI relies on specialized hardware, such as GPUs (Graphics Processing Units) and TPUs (Tensor Processing Units), which are energy-intensive to produce.

Rapid advancements in AI mean frequent hardware upgrades, leading to an increase in e-waste as old equipment is discarded.

Huge Data Collection and Storage: AI systems rely on large amounts of data, which needs to be stored and processed continuously. Storing and managing this data requires vast server farms, further increasing energy consumption and environmental load.

Impact: AI brings dual challenges. AI may optimize operations in industry wide use case, while these applications frequently require a lot of processing power, which could offset the energy savings they provide through increased operational effectiveness.

As AI adoption and influence grows, but it brings many challenges to our economy, society, and personal relationships, so it highlights the need for ethical AI principles—guidelines that ensure AI is used responsibly, transparently, and fairly. Ethical AI principles emphasize values like privacy, accountability, and inclusivity, aiming to protect human rights and promote societal well-being.

At same time, governments, organizations, and international bodies are responding by developing AI governance frameworks that promote ethical principles. These frameworks deal with things like minimizing bias, safeguarding data, and making sure AI decisions are transparent. By bringing AI developments accordance with human values, ethical standards foster confidence and guarantee that AI is used ethically and fairly for the benefit of everyone.

Ethical Principles and Frameworks

There are ethical challenges or concerns about how these AI systems are developed and used, including issues like lack of transparency, bias, privacy, security, safety, etc., as we discussed in detail in the above section. These risks have made regulators more eager to establish rules to protect against potential harm while still encouraging innovation. The goal is to create consistent Principles and Frameworks that promote responsible and safe AI development and deployment. The focus is now on determining the best way to implement these regulations.

These Ethical Principals and framework are essential to help organizations to use AI responsibly and build trust with users. We will try to understand the AI Ethical Principals to overcome the AI Ethical Challenges as depicted below.

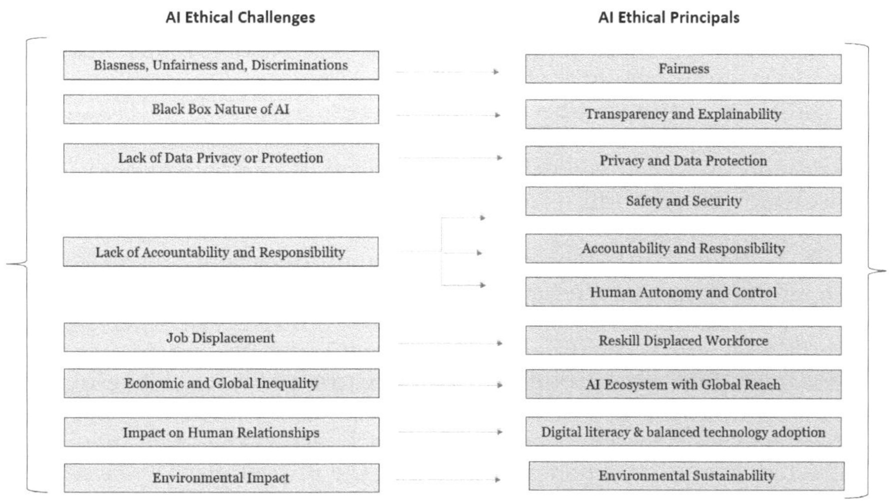

Figure 2.3: AI Ethical Principal and frameworks

1. Fairness

Fairness in AI applications mean, it must treat all users and groups impartially and fairly. Objective of this principal to overcome the challenge raised as biasness, unfairness and discrimination by AI applications.
It involves developing and deploying AI models that can make judgments or forecasts without favoring any person or demographic group based on attributes like age, gender, race, demographic or other traits. The goal is to make sure that the AI treats everyone fairly, providing equal accuracy, benefits and quality of service regardless of a person's background or identity.

To address the biasness, unfairness and discrimination challenges with AI applications, please find below the approaches & key elements involved in ensuring fairness.

Inclusive Design: Engage diverse teams in the creation and development of AI systems such as social scientists, humanists, and other relevant experts. This brings in a variety of perspectives and helps minimize the risk of missing issues that could impact specific groups. Design your AI algorithms with the goal of achieving fairness.

Fairness Metric: These are quantitative tools used to measure whether the AI model treats different groups fairly. Since fairness in AI is complex, different metrics are used based on the use case or situation.

Diverse Training Data: AI models learn from historical data, and if this data lacks diversity, the model may reflect existing biases. Ensuring diverse datasets helps reduce biased outcomes.

Diverse Data Collection: AI System should be trained from the diverse datasets. Plan that representative and varied samples from every demographic are included in the data used to train AI models. By doing this, biases that can produce unfair results are less likely.

Bias Audits and Fairness Checks: Conduct regular audits to detect and correct biases in AI models. Ensures that AI outcomes are fair and transparent, especially in sensitive real-world applications. For Example - A financial institution could audit its loan approval algorithm to ensure it is not biased against minorities.

Fairness Notions: This concept means equal treatment, regardless of their background or characteristics. The idea is that all individuals should have the same experience and outcome, with no group getting special treatment.

Equity: While equal treatment means treating everyone the same, **equity** recognizes that some groups may need extra support to achieve fair outcomes. It involves adjusting policies or decisions to address existing disadvantages.

Feedback and Engagement: Get user feedback, especially from marginalized or affected groups, and better understand the impact of AI systems and make necessary adjustments.

2. Transparency and Explainability

The openness and clarity with which an AI system or AI decision-making mechanism functions, is referred as transparency. Transparency in the context of AI, refers as giving clear explanations of how an AI system operates, what data it consumes, and how it draws conclusions.

Explainability is the ability of an AI system to provide human-understandable explanations for its actions and results. It guarantees that people understand the reasoning behind a certain decision, which is necessary for responsibility and trust. This principle is targeting to make the current black box nature of the AI System a White Box nature. Overcoming AI explainability and transparency challenges requires a combination of technical, organizational, and regulatory strategies. Here are approaches that can help address these challenges and build trust in AI Applications.

Use of Explainable AI (XAI) Models/tools: Implementing Explainable AI (XAI) techniques involve using methods that clarify how AI models reach their decisions, making complex algorithms interpretable and accessible to users. By providing insights into AI's decision-making process—such as highlighting key factors influencing outcomes—XAI helps end users understand and trust AI, leading to more informed and confident use of AI applications.

Transparent Model Documentation (AI Fact Sheets): To improve transparency, Transparent Model Documentation (AI Fact Sheets) entail producing thorough documentation for AI models. Usually, these "fact sheets" contain crucial details like the model purpose, data sources, design, constraints, and any biases of the model. AI Fact Sheets foster confidence and facilitate more responsible deployment and supervision of AI systems by giving stakeholders an understandable, easily available summary of the AI's capabilities and any known limitations.

Balancing Transparency and Intellectual Property: Sharing enough information about AI models to promote accountability and trust while avoiding disclosing and Intellectual or sensitive information is part of striking a balance between transparency and intellectual property. By revealing the model's goal, data sources, and performance indicators while safeguarding certain algorithms, methods, or trade secrets that give an advantage over competitors, this balance can be attained. This method promotes openness and moral principles without sacrificing intellectual property by enabling stakeholders to comprehend the model's capabilities and constraints.

3. Privacy and Data Protection:

AI systems should respect people's privacy and safeguard personal information from misuse and illegal access. To preserve public trust, AI system should respect people's rights, Individual 's privacy must be protected.

Here are techniques to safeguard Privacy and Data Protection

Data Encryption: Sensitive information is protected using data encryption, which transforms the data into unreadable format that only authorized individuals with the right decryption key may access or decode. Data is safe and unreadable even if it is intercepted or accessed by unauthorized persons thanks to encryption. Organizations may secure privacy, adhere to data protection laws, and lower the risk of data breaches in AI applications by implementing encryption approaches to data both in transit and at rest.

Anonymization & Pseudonymization: Anonymization eliminates or modifies or masks personal information so that it cannot be linked back. Once data is anonymized, it can't be re-identified, so people's privacy is fully protected.

Pseudonymization replaces identifying information (like names or IDs) with fake identifiers, such as codes. This can add a layer of privacy protection.

Access Control and Role-Based Permissions: Using Access Control, access can be restricted to personal data within an AI system so that only authorized individuals can view or use it.

Using role-based permissions (e.g., data analyst, developer), organizations ensure that sensitive data is only accessible to those who need it, enhancing data privacy and security while minimizing the risk of unauthorized access.

Data Minimization and Limited Retention Policies: By limiting the amount of sensitive or personal data collection, you may reduce the chance of needless data exposure. AI systems should only be trained on the intended and essential data.

User Consent and Control: User Consent ensures that individuals are informed about how their personal data will be collected, used, and shared. Users must give explicit consent before their data is processed, allowing them to make informed choices about their privacy.

Additionally, providing users with control over their data—such as the ability to access, modify, or delete their information—empowers them and reinforces their trust in the system.

By prioritizing user consent and control, organizations can comply with data protection regulations.

Differential Privacy: This method protects privacy by adding random noise to data, making individual contributions untraceable while ensuring that the output of data analysis remains statistically accurate. This method is commonly used in AI and machine learning where aggregated insights are needed without revealing individual data points.

Compliance with Data Protection Regulations: Governments and regulators have introduced data privacy laws (like the General Data Protection Regulations (**GDPR**) and the California Consumer Privacy Act (**CCPA**) to protect users. However, AI systems must align with these rules, adding complexity to how data is collected, used, and shared.

4. AI Safe Application

AI systems operate as intended, even in the face of adversarial threats or attacks. It's vital to solve safety and security problems before implementing AI in critical applications.

Here are techniques to measure safe AI applications

Adversarial learning is an AI technique in which a model (often referred to as the "adversary") creates false inputs, or adversarial examples, to attack another model. The main objective is to increase its security and robustness by exposing the target model to potential vulnerabilities during training,

Adversarial testing is a technique used in AI and machine learning research to assess how a system or model responds to malicious or tricky inputs intended to take advantage of its vulnerabilities. The main objective of adversarial testing is to find and fix vulnerabilities, which is carried out prior to the AI system being used in practical situations.

Fail-Safe Mechanisms: AI Safety measures are design strategies that guarantee AI systems stay safe and stable even in the face of unforeseen problems or mistakes. The goal is to prevent AI from causing harm or from acting in a way that could have unfavorable effects.

Anomaly Detection: Using AI itself to keep an eye on system activity and look for odd trends that could point to a malfunction or security risk. This makes it possible to identify and address possible dangers quickly.

5. Accountable and Responsible AI Application:

It implies that the people who develop and deploy AI systems should have accountability for the actions and decisions those systems undertake.

Here are a few recommendations to *build accountability and responsibility for AI Applications.*

Collaborative Governance: Encourage collaboration between developers, businesses, and regulators to align accountability practices with emerging AI technologies.

Guidelines for Responsibility: Establish accountability frameworks that define specific roles and responsibilities for developers, companies, users, and regulators.

Implement policies to ensure that companies deploying AI remain liable for its failures, regardless of technical issues.

Regulatory Frameworks for AI Liability: Governments should establish laws for AI liability that clarify who is accountable in complex AI-driven systems.

Mandatory audits of AI systems can ensure compliance with safety and security standards.

6. Human Autonomy and Control:

It is essential to understand the role that humans have in autonomy and control over AI. This idea highlights how essential it is to maintain human oversight, decision-making authority, and the capacity to interfere with AI processes, particularly in sensitive or critical scenarios. Here's a detailed exploration of this role:

Human Intervention and Control: AI Systems and technologies should be supervised and directed by humans to guarantee that they function within ethical and practical bounds. In addition to ensuring that AI technologies are used responsibly and successfully, human oversight helps to preserve responsibility.

Human-in-the-Loop (HITL): By directly integrating human decision-makers into the AI operating loop, this method enables them to examine and approve decisions prior to their execution. For instance, in autonomous vehicles, human drivers might have the final say in navigating complex situations that AI might not fully understand.

Human-on-the-Loop (HOTL): This paradigm does not require constant human supervision, but it does give humans the capacity to supervise AI decisions and intervene when needed. It's common in semi-autonomous systems where AI handles routine tasks, but humans manage exceptions.

7. Reskilled Workers

While AI will replace some jobs, it also creates new opportunities that require human expertise. Organizations deploying AI systems must take ethical responsibility for the impact on their workforce. To minimize the impacts, Organization should reskill their workforce for AI related Roles.

Here are a few approaches to overcome this challenge.

Invest in Reskilling & Upskilling Programs: Offer training programs that teach displaced workers AI-adjacent skills (e.g., data management, AI system monitoring, and prompt engineering). Provide free or subsidized courses in partnership with educational institutions to help workers transition to new roles.

Facilitate Transitions into AI-Related Roles: Encourage displaced employees to pursue careers in emerging fields related to AI Roles as Prompt engineers, Data scientists and analysts, AI Trainer, Ethics officers etc.

The challenge lies in ensuring that displaced workers can access these new opportunities through proper training and support.

8. AI Ecosystem with Global Reach

To harness AI as a force for global good, policymakers, businesses, and international organizations must work together to create an inclusive AI ecosystem.

Here are some ways to reduce global inequality:

Investment in Digital Infrastructure: International organizations, such as the World Bank and the United Nations, should support low-income countries in developing digital infrastructure, enabling them to participate in the global AI economy.

AI for Social Good Initiatives: Governments and corporations should fund AI solutions that address pressing global challenges—such as healthcare, agriculture, and climate change—in underserved regions.

Inclusive Policies and Fair Competition: Policymakers must ensure that the economic benefits of AI are distributed. Regulations should prevent dominant behavior by large corporations and encourage competition by supporting startups and small businesses.

Global Knowledge Sharing and Collaboration: Partnerships between wealthy and developing countries can promote the exchange of research, best practices, and AI technologies. This can help bridge the gap in capabilities.

Education and Skills Development: Governments and educational institutions must prioritize digital literacy and AI skills for all populations. This includes providing free or low-cost AI training programs to empower people in underserved regions.

9. Digital literacy balanced technology adoption

A balanced approach to technology adoption and digital literacy are crucial for mitigating the possible harm that artificial intelligence may cause to human relationships. These methods assist individuals develop AI-driven interactions without sacrificing true human connection by raising awareness, encouraging responsible use, and integrating AI thoughtfully into daily life.

Digital literacy refers to the knowledge and skills needed to understand, use, and engage with digital technologies in a responsible and informed way.

Balanced technology adoption involves integrating AI and other digital technologies into our lives in a way that enhances human experience without overshadowing human interactions:

Understanding AI's Influence: Educating people on how AI affects decision-making, recommendations, and preferences in subtle ways. For instance, people are better able to make thoughtful decisions that represent their true interests when they are aware of how AI recommendation systems operate on social media.

Mindful Usage: Motivating individuals to use technology purposefully, particularly in social settings, and to put in-person connections ahead of online interactions whenever feasible.

Recognizing and Setting Boundaries with AI Companions: Teaching people about the limitations of AI companions, particularly for vulnerable populations (such as young or elderly users), and assisting them in realizing that although AI can mimic connection, it cannot take the place of human connections

Complementing, Not Replacing, Human Interaction: AI technologies and digital solutions should be designed to enhance interpersonal interactions and community involvement, not to replace human interaction. AI friends may, for instance, recommend social gatherings or remind users to stay in touch with their loved ones, assisting in striking a balance between virtual and in-person relationships.

10. Environmental Sustainability

AI development and operation require significant computational resources, which leads to significant energy consumption and carbon emissions, particularly when training large models. This has raised questions regarding AI's impact on the environment, especially considering the growing need for AI-driven solutions.

Sustainability is a growing need to remediate the negative impact of AI on the environment using the below considerations during AI development and deployment. It is a fundamental aspect in the interest of Society and Human benefits. Here are below remediation pointers for environmental sustainability as

a) **Energy-Efficient Algorithms:** It is recommended to design and implement more energy efficient AI Algorithms to reduce the need of computational power and lead to less energy consumption.

b) **Model Optimization:** Model optimization techniques are critical for improving the efficiency of AI models, reducing their computational and energy requirements, and enhancing performance. Some common techniques

Pruning: It is important to remove the less important parameters from neural network, this can result in small and efficient model with minimal loss in accuracy.

Quantization: Reducing the precision of the numbers used in the model's computations, such as converting 32-bit floating-point numbers to 8-bit integers, which can significantly reduce the model's size and speed up inference.

Distillation: Transferring knowledge from a larger, complex model (teacher) to a smaller, simpler model (student) that is more efficient while maintaining comparable performance.

c) **Sustainable Hardware Design and Data centers:** Sustainable Data Centers: Reducing the environmental impact of data centers can be achieved by using renewable energy sources such as solar, wind, or hydroelectric power and upgrading cooling systems. Sustainable Hardware Design: Creating hardware that is energy-efficient and specially tuned for AI functions can help reduce power consumption.

Overall focus on developing AI technologies with minimal environmental impact, often referred to as "Green AI."

Potential Solutions to Mitigate AI's Environmental Impact

1. **Improving Energy Efficiency**:

Developing Low-Power Models: Research and development of energy-efficient algorithms and models that perform tasks with less computation can reduce energy consumption. Techniques like model pruning, quantization, and knowledge distillation can make models more efficient.

Using Renewable Energy Sources: Encourage data centers to transition to renewable energy sources, such as solar or wind, to power their operations and reduce carbon emissions.

2. **Optimizing Data Center Cooling and Design**:

Efficient Cooling Solutions: Innovations in data center cooling, such as liquid cooling or building centers in naturally cooler regions, can reduce the energy used for temperature control.

Eco-Friendly Data Centers: Building eco-friendly data centers that use sustainable materials and energy-efficient design principles can help mitigate the environmental impact.

3. **Encouraging Model Sharing and Reuse**:

Pre-trained Models: Encouraging researchers and developers to use existing pre-trained models rather than retraining large models from scratch can help reduce redundant computation.

Federated and Distributed Learning: Decentralized approaches like federated learning can allow models to be trained across multiple devices without centralizing all data, reducing the need for extensive data storage and transfer.

4. **Promoting Sustainable AI Practices**:

Green AI Research: Supporting research into "Green AI," which prioritizes environmental sustainability in model development and deployment.

Environmental Accountability: Encouraging companies and organizations to assess the environmental impact of their AI projects, publicly disclose their energy usage and carbon footprint, and adopt sustainability goals.

5. **Advocating for AI in Environmental Applications**:

While AI itself consumes resources, it also holds the potential to aid environmental efforts, such as optimizing energy grids, monitoring ecosystems, and supporting conservation efforts. By directing AI research toward sustainable applications, we can offset some of its environmental footprint.

Conclusion

In this chapter, we have understood in detail, the various AI ethical challenges like biasness, black box nature of AI, data privacy and protection issue, accountability and responsibility issue, economic and global inequality, impact of Human relationship, impact on environment etc. We have also understood that organizations need ethical principal and guidelines in their AI adoption journey. In the next chapter, we are going to talk about the security risk & threats around AI system. As AI Systems going through massive innovations journey, hackers are trying to figure out the loophole in the AI system so AI Developer and deployer needs to be ready against these adversarial attacks, protecting data, bad prompts, hate, hallucinations etc.

Chapter 3

AI Security: Threats and Solutions

Chapter 1 discussed the various use cases or industries where AI can bring about significant transformation. Another such area is cyber security, where AI plays a critical role. For Example, AI algorithms can analyze massive amounts of data to detect patterns indicative of a cyber threat. They can also scan the entire network for weaknesses to prevent common kinds of cyberattacks.
At the same time, cybersecurity threats in AI are diverse and evolving, targeting different aspects of AI systems, from data and models to the supply chain. Sophisticated hackers, an expanding attack surface, an explosion of data, and growing infrastructure complexity make it further difficult to safeguard data, manage user access, and quickly detect and respond to AI security threats. Organizations must adopt robust security measures to mitigate these threats, including secure AI development practices, regular audits, and continuous monitoring of deployed AI systems.

This chapter focuses on the threats or security challenges for an AI application and potential solutions.

In this chapter, we will cover the following aspects of AI security.

- Importance of security for AI applications
- AI-specific vulnerabilities
- GenAI and Agentic AI-specific vulnerabilities
- Cybersecurity threats in AI
- Protecting AI systems from adversarial attacks
- Ensuring data integrity and confidentiality

Importance of security for AI applications

Like any other software application, security is critical for AI applications. AI applications deal with a lot of information, may involve higher costs compared to normal applications, and may also have complex insights. A security breach in AI applications can pose multiple risks at an individual, organization, or geographic level, as described below.

- **Information Theft**: AI applications often handle sensitive information, and a security breach could result in unauthorized access and theft of this information, leading to multiple compliance issues and risks. Information theft at any level, individual/organization/geography level, can compromise identity, which may lead to financial Loss and reputational damage. For Example, at the individual level, it may compromise personal relationships and cause emotional distress. At the organizational level, it may compromise intellectual property, customer data, and business operations, potentially resulting in system downtime and Loss of competitive advantage. At the geographical level, Information theft is dangerous for governments because it can compromise national security, lead to financial Loss, and erode public trust. It can also result in the misuse of sensitive information, such as classified documents or personal data, and potentially disrupt government operations, geopolitical relations, and other complex issues among governments.
- **System Theft**: Malicious actors might manipulate AI systems, causing them to produce inaccurate decisions or predictions, which could have serious repercussions. For Example, at the individual level, system theft can aid in the compromise of personal information, such as passwords and login credentials, leading to financial Loss, personal reputation loss, or even privacy theft. At the organizational level, it can compromise intellectual property, customer data, and business operations, potentially resulting in system downtime and Loss of competitive advantage, reputation, or finance. At the geographical level, system theft can compromise national security, put pressure on government operations, and break public trust.

In summary, information theft or system theft for AI applications can lead to

- Reputation Loss by damaging the organization's reputation using the AI application or individuals involved in the design and delivery of the application or even geographies using the application.
- Financial Loss to the individual due to unauthorized access to financial data or to the organizations due to legal penalties, system unavailability, and possible litigation/ compliance issues.
- Intellectual Property loss leads to Loss or theft of valuable intellectual property. Many times, AI applications have a good amount of intellectual property.

- Privacy Loss results in Loss of privacy for individuals, organizations, or governments, depending on the level of usage.

Another major challenge is that once an attacker gains access to an AI system, it may be used as a lethal weapon to accelerate further attacks on similar systems or integrated systems, making the Loss multi-fold. Hence, it is important to understand the threats to AI applications and potential ways to mitigate them to avoid Loss and minimize risk. In the next section, let's discuss vulnerabilities specific to AI applications.

AI Application-Specific Vulnerabilities

Like any standard software application, the AI system's design, implementation, configuration, or operation could have inherent issues, as this field is still evolving, practices are still being established, and developers and designers have yet to learn from the worst. AI has the potential to generate malware that could evade detection by current security filters, but only if it is trained on quality exploit data. There is a realistic possibility that highly capable states have repositories of malware that are large enough to effectively train an AI model for this purpose. Similarly, in Generative AI, prompt Injection is the most significant threat to any Large language model. It ranks as the number one vulnerability in OWASP's top ten for Large language model applications, ***https://owasp.org/www-project-top-10-for-large-language-model-applications/***.

The news articles about how a car dealership incorporated LLM into their chatbot, and a user was able to trick it into selling him a car for $1.
Some of the reasons why AI applications are highly vulnerable are described below.

- **Complexity of AI Systems**: AI systems often use deep learning techniques. These models can sometimes be difficult to understand and analyze, making it challenging to identify security vulnerabilities. In addition, many AI models are opaque, making it difficult to understand how they make decisions.
- **Data Quality and Availability**: AI systems sometimes need large amounts of high-quality training data, which may not always be available or reliable. In certain industries or applications, a lack of proper quality data can compromise AI systems.
- Regulatory and Compliance Challenges: Security regulations around AI applications are still evolving, and there are no clear guidelines for AI security. At the same time, AI systems must comply with various regulations, such as APRA (Australian Prudential Regulation Authority), General Data Protection Regulation (GDPR), and Health Insurance Portability and Accountability Act (HIPAA), which can be challenging to navigate.
- **Limited Resources**: AI security often requires significant investment or specialized personnel, which may not be feasible or readily available for all organizations.

All of these factors increase the complexity of AI applications and contribute to making them vulnerable to adversarial attacks that compromise their security. Further, coding, misconfigurations, outdated software, weakly implemented access controls, or human error can introduce potential vulnerabilities in AI applications.

Various types of vulnerabilities seen in AI applications are described below.

- **Data Breaches**: AI models rely on large volumes of data to learn and improve their performance. This data must be carefully curated to include labeled instances of the types of events that the AI is designed to detect. Another challenge is that AI models need examples of normal and malicious patterns to learn from. Training data often contains sensitive information about customers, business operations, and other critical aspects of an organization. Storing and using this data to train AI models increases the risk of data breach, which can have severe consequences. Example: AI for Network Traffic Analysis. AI models designed to identify threats in network traffic need training data that includes examples of both normal traffic patterns and malicious traffic patterns (e.g., DDoS attacks, malware), which may contain sensitive information about customers, business operations, and network infrastructure.
- **Adversarial Attacks:** AI systems are designed to create models that aid in accomplishing specific objectives. For instance, an AI system can be instructed to distinguish between harmless files and potential malware in network traffic. This gives malicious cyber attackers an opportunity to train their own AI systems to learn the models of defensive ones. Further, it could enable the attackers to uncover methods to bypass the AI system by identifying means to uncover the model's weaknesses and use it to harm rather than benefit others.
- **Data Manipulation and Data Poisoning**: Data manipulation and poisoning attacks focus on tampering with the labeled data used to train AI models. Attackers insert incorrectly labeled examples into the dataset to mislead the model during training. For instance, if malicious traffic is mislabeled as benign in the training data, the AI model will fail to identify such attacks. This allows attackers to bypass the security of the AI system once it is deployed.
- **Bias and Discrimination**: An AI model's effectiveness depends heavily on the quality of its training data. These models learn by being exposed to numerous labelled inputs and developing patterns to generate the desired outcomes. However, a key issue with this approach is that biased training data leads to biased AI models. A common example is facial recognition systems, frequently trained on images from specific demographic groups. As a result, these systems tend to exhibit significantly higher error rates for individuals not represented in the training data.
- **Model Supply Chain Attacks:** Training an AI model is a complex task that requires gathering a vast amount of labeled data and leveraging it to train the model. This process demands access to large datasets and machine learning

and data science expertise. Consequently, many organizations use AI models developed and trained by third parties. However, this introduces the risk that attackers could target the model developers, potentially injecting malicious data or taking other actions to compromise the model.

In summary, while many vulnerabilities exist for AI applications, it is also important to note that AI applications play an increasingly vital role in decision-making and data processing in the current era. Hence, maintaining the integrity and confidentiality of AI applications is of paramount importance to reduce the risk of vulnerabilities.

GenAI and Agentic AI Application Specific Vulnerabilities

With the evolution of AI technology, concepts such as GenAI and AgenticAI have received significant adoption in the industry. GenAI (GenerativeAI) helps automate tasks, and agenticAI provides a strategic approach to automating and orchestrating complex business workflows with the help of AI agents. Large Language Models (LLMs) are the core of these applications. By attacking the application architecture components surrounding the LLMs, and specifically the guardrails, hackers can easily manipulate or disrupt the logical chain of the system, taking these components out of sync with the intended data flow, or otherwise exploiting them, or, in turn, manipulating the interaction between these components in the logical chain of the application implementation apart from manipulating the LLMs itself as described below.

Most of the vulnerabilities applicable to AI applications hold good for LLMs, as detailed in subsequent sections. The impact of these vulnerabilities on LLMs is captured below.

- **Data poisoning:** Attackers can manipulate the data used to train an LLM model, making it difficult for the model to provide accurate results.
- **Denial of service:** Attackers can interact with an LLM in a way that consumes a lot of resources, which can negatively impact the quality of service provided by the LLM, impacting the users.
- **Supply chain vulnerabilities:** Many organizations use open-source components, outdated pre-trained LLM models, or corrupted training data sets, which makes supply chains vulnerable.
- **Sensitive information disclosure:** LLMs' accidental disclosure of confidential data in the response can lead to privacy violations, security breaches, or compliance issues.
- **Insecure output handling:** If LLM outputs are not validated properly, they may lead to risks like privilege escalation and website security flaws such as cross-site scripting (**XSS**), Cross-side request forgery(**CSRF**), and Server-side

request forgery(**SSRF**), which can lead to unauthorized access, data leakage, and even remote code execution.

- **Insecure plugin design:** Designing in-secured plugins for LLMs can compromise the entire system.
- **Excessive agency:** Sometimes, LLMs are overloaded with functionalities, permissions, or autonomy, resulting in damaging actions in response to unexpected outputs.
- **Overreliance:** Due to the nature of LLMs, people or systems can sometimes be heavily dependent on them without proper human oversight, leading to security vulnerabilities and misinformation.

Especially for agentic AI applications, a combination of Flow breaking, Prompt Injection, and jailbreaking are AI attack vectors that have surfaced that can manipulate the AI workflows. Flow breaking can be compared to the race condition in traditional software application security. It is an AI attack against the implementation and architecture of LLM applications and agentic systems. User inputs and generated model outputs can adversely affect the broader system's other components. Prompt Injection can concatenate untrusted user input with a trusted prompt, adversely impacting the application output. Jailbreaking can exploit safety filters built into LLMs.

Like agentic AI-related vulnerabilities, a few vulnerabilities that have surfaced for Generative AI applications are

- **Forbidden information**: A design flaw or loophole in the system where the system bypasses rules around data sharing, especially when the data is short or transmitted quickly, leading to forbidden information to clients.
- In many cases, due to system flaws or race conditions, a guardrail was not finished before the content was streamed to the user.
- **Software exploitation**: Exploiting the software components used in the system, especially when a component is overwhelmed, impacting other components in the data flow.
- **Order of operations**: Due to design flaws, certain components are skipped or not processed in the intended order, leading to unintended results or bypassing critical business rules.

To address some of these issues, the output of LLMs and applications using GenAI or agentic need to be monitored carefully, especially in instances such as second thoughts where a system retracts answers or recovers results. When a user clicks the stop button while the answer is still streaming, the system should pause and revert. Further, the following design practices can help limit some of these issues.

- **Immediate Validation**: Systems should ensure data is checked and validated even before streaming begins. If any validation is missed, this should be captured, and an appropriate alert should be raised.
- **Rate Limiting**: Strict rate and size restrictions should be applied to prevent data leaks.

- **Real-Time Monitoring**: Tools to monitor for unusual patterns in data streams and pipelines should be incorporated to help identify proactive issues.
- **Throttling and Timeouts**: Introducing delays or stop mechanisms during data transmission for transmissions identified as suspicious could help.
- **Secure Design Practices**: Validating and testing systems, especially for edge cases where data streams might bypass controls due to length or speed, can help address issues related to the order of operation or forbidden information.

In summary, some of the vulnerabilities related to generative AI or agentic AI applications can be minimized through secure design practices, appropriate monitoring tools, and thorough testing.

The next section discusses potential cybersecurity threats in AI.

Cybersecurity threats in AI

The revolutionizing power of AI applications comes with significant security risks and vulnerabilities.Traditionally, cybersecurity (cyber-security) refers to ways and means to secure cyber areas that may include computers, devices, or applications related to Information technology. It encompasses a wide range of technologies, processes, and practices designed to safeguard information and ensure the integrity, confidentiality, and availability of data in the digital realm. Interestingly, While AI plays a very important role in defending com, rs, servers, mobile devices, electronic systems, networks, and data from malicious attacks, there are multiple cybersecurity threats for AI applications to AI applications themselves. Cybersecurity is critical as it involves protecting sensitive data, complying with regulations, ensuring business continuity, and establishing trust in the system.

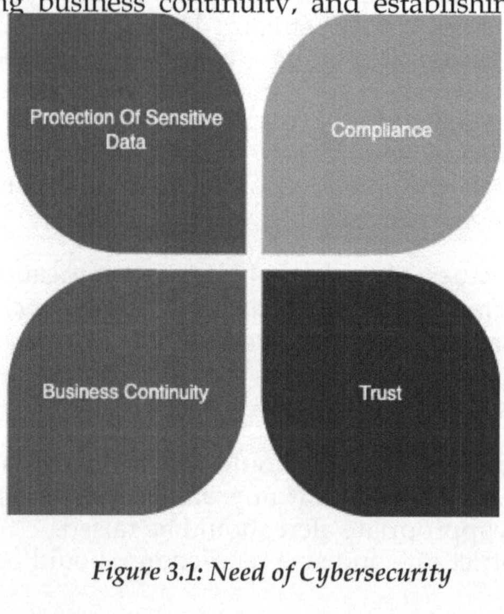

Figure 3.1: Need of Cybersecurity

- **Protection of Sensitive Data:** Though all applications need to protect themselves, this becomes more critical for AI-based applications, as the foundation of AI applications is information or data. In AI applications, identifying and protecting personal, financial, and proprietary information from theft and misuse is of paramount importance.
- **Compliance:** The regulations around the Use of AI applications are still evolving, so there are no clear compliance guidelines. However, like any standard software application, AI applications should align with regulatory requirements for data protection, such as GDPR, HIPAA, and PCI DSS, to name a few.
-
- **Business Continuity:** AI applications are often the backbone of critical business operations or business applications. Any disruptions to these applications could lead to financial Loss, reputational damage, operational downtime, and related Loss.
-
- **Trust:** AI applications sometimes use complex algorithms to provide meaningful insights into data. Techniques such as deep learning help maintain customer and stakeholder confidence in an organization's ability to arrive at these insights. Any compromise in these systems directly impacts the trust.

The core components of cybersecurity and their impact on AI applications are described below:

Core Components of Cybersecurity

In this section, we will discuss the Core Components of Cybersecurity (Fig 3.2)

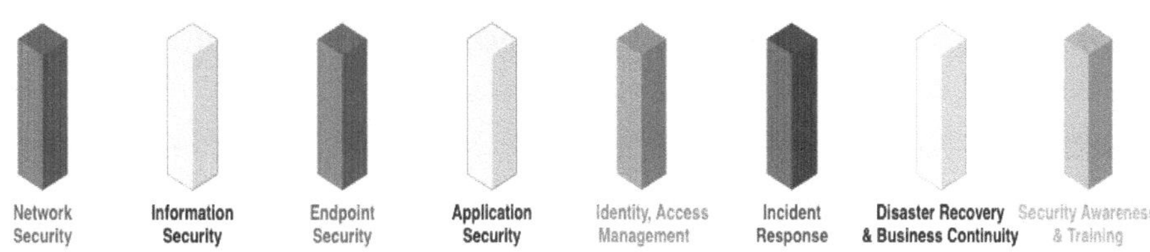

Figure 3.2: Core components of Cybersecurity overview

- **Network Security:** Network security refers to protecting data's integrity, confidentiality, and availability as it is transmitted across or accessed from a network. In standard applications, various network components such as firewalls, intrusion detection systems (IDS), and virtual private networks (VPNs) are used. Due to the nature and complexity associated with AI applications, the resulting network security-related threats become threatening. Some standard threats, such as Denial of Service (DoS) attacks, can overwhelm AI systems, making them unavailable. Similarly, another threat is the interception of communication between AI systems to inject malicious data or man-in-the-middle (MitM) attacks. To prevent AI applications from such issues, it is important to adopt threat identification Techniques, including

- o continuously monitoring and analyzing network traffic to detect any suspicious activity
- o identifying unusual patterns in network traffic or system behavior
- o identifying potential vulnerabilities in AI systems and networks
- o adopting testing techniques such as penetration testing that can simulate attacks on AI systems to validate their defenses

- **Information Security:** Information security refers to protecting information itself, regardless of where it is stored, whether on a local device, in the cloud, or Transit. Multiple information security risks must be addressed in AI applications to ensure the confidentiality, integrity, and availability of data, models, and systems. As described in the previous section, issues like data poisoning, data eavesdropping, and data inference make this more complex.

Just not data: AI models have multiple risks, as described below.

- o **Model Inversion**: Cyber attackers can reverse engineer AI models to extract sensitive information.
- o **Model Theft**: If proper security access control is not implemented, AI models can be accessed or replicated unauthorizedly.
- o **Model Manipulation**: Cyber attackers can easily manipulate AI models intentionally to deceive or mislead, which can have unwanted consequences.

Another common thing is SQL injection, where malicious SQL code is injected to extract or modify sensitive data.
To address these, various techniques can be used to protect information, including data encryption, secure storage solutions, and access control measures, as explained in the last section of this chapter.

- **Endpoint Security:** Endpoint security protects individual devices that connect to a network, such as computers, smartphones, and tablets, from threats. Various techniques used in the industry to provide endpoint security are Antivirus software, endpoint detection and response (EDR), and mobile device management (MDM) solutions. The antivirus software or EDR techniques must be kept up-to-date and tested for AI applications.
- **Application Security:** In the case of AI applications, application security refers to securing them by identifying, fixing, and protecting them against vulnerabilities. This can be achieved only by adopting secure coding practices, performing regular application updates, and using application firewalls. AI application security is a complex and rapidly evolving field, with several bottlenecks that hinder the development of secure AI systems. Some of the key ones are described below.
- **Lack of Standardization**: Since the field of AI is evolving, there is yet to be a

defined framework or policy for standardization.

- **Inconsistent security frameworks**: Different AI applications and industries have varying security standards, making it challenging to develop universally applicable security solutions.
- **Inadequate testing and validation**: Lack of proper testing practice for AI systems specifically leads to potential breaches. AI applications are often not thoroughly tested for security vulnerabilities,
- **Insufficient Human Oversight**: Many times, due to a lack of skills, awareness, time, or even cost, there is not sufficient human oversight involved in validating AI models. This increases the risk of security breaches.

  Limited human expertise: AI security requires specialized knowledge, often in short supply. Hence, standardization, appropriate testing, sufficient training on AI application best practices, and human oversight are critical for the success of AI applications.

- **Identity and Access Management (IAM):** Identity and access management refers to user identity management and resource access control based on roles, permissions, and policies. Multiple technologies, such as multi-factor authentication (MFA), single sign-on (SSO), and role-based access control (RBAC), can be adopted to address these issues.
- **Incident Response:** Incident response for AI applications refers to preparing for, detecting, and responding to cybersecurity incidents, such as breaches or attacks. Hence, AI applications must use techniques such as Incident response plans, forensic analysis, and breach notification procedures to address these.
- **Disaster Recovery and Business Continuity (DR & BC):** DR & BC refers to ensuring that an organization can continue to operate and recover quickly in the event of a cyberattack, natural disaster, or other disruptions. For AI applications, it is important to implement techniques such as Backup solutions, recovery plans, and redundancy strategies to address these needs.
- **Security Awareness and Training:** Security awareness and training refers to educating employees and stakeholders about cybersecurity threats and best practices to reduce human error, which is often a key vulnerability. This includes Phishing simulation exercises, security awareness programs, and regular training sessions.

Now that we understand the core components of cybersecurity and why they are important for AI applications, we will describe below the various types of cybersecurity threats found in industry.

- **Malware** is malicious software designed by intruders, also called hackers, to harm or exploit systems by stealing or damaging data. Examples include Viruses, worms, ransomware, and spyware. AI can allow malware to dynamically adjust its tactics during an attack based on real-time analysis of the target's defences. For Example,
- using AI applications, criminals can create multiple malware new variants of malware quickly and automatically through automated code generation.

This helps them create many different attacks with different characteristics but similar functionality. Running malware and security software against each other can teach AI systems how malware is detected. They can then modify the malware to avoid detection or generate new evasion Techniques. Even GenAI adapts to security systems and can learn from the results of other attacks.

- **Phishing:** In the case of phishing, attackers deceive people to obtain sensitive information by pretending to be a trustworthy entity or installing malware such as viruses, worms, ransomware, etc. Examples include **fake** emails, fraudulent websites, and social engineering attacks. It is easy to generate free hacker tools like WormGPT or FraudGPT – a dark version of the OpenAI tool using AI. These tools can generate requests to create phishing emails, generate code to spoof specific websites, or any other number of nefarious requests, making it much easier for hackers or attackers.
- **Denial of Service (DoS) Attacks:** Attacks aimed at overwhelming a system or network to make it unavailable to users. **Examples** include Distributed Denial of Service (DDoS) attacks, botnets, etc. With AI, it is easy to read and analyze patterns of a compromised server or system, and there is an excessive number of illegitimate requests from seemingly valid users. Attackers identify vulnerable computer systems that they can infect with malicious attacks, mass-infection campaigns, and other activities like identity theft and automate all these at a fingertip.
- **Man-in-the-Middle (MitM) Attacks:** Attacks where an attacker intercepts and potentially alters communication between two parties without their knowledge. **Examples** include Eavesdropping on network traffic or session hijacking applications, which can easily detect patterns in network traffic and potential loopholes to aid in MitM attacks.
- **Insider Threats:** Threats posed by individuals within an organization, such as employees or contractors, who misuse their access. This could include data theft, sabotage, and unintentional data breaches. **For Example,** a poorly configured URL within a GitHub repository dedicated to AI models unintentionally exposed 38TB of data. The data included sensitive information such as passwords and internal messages. Though this involved data theft of an AI application, again, AI can aid in insider threats as it can process a large amount of information or identify data patterns.
- **Advanced Persistent Threats (APTs):** Sophisticated and targeted cyberattacks where an intruder gains access to a network and remains undetected for an extended period while inside or accessing the system without the actual owner's knowledge. **Examples** include State-sponsored espionage and the targeting of critical infrastructure. These threats pose more risks to AI applications than normal applications, as the fundamental of AI systems is to learn from the behavior of system data or patterns. Unfortunately, this helps cyber criminals train their own AI systems on malware and other malicious software to 'level up' their attacks. With the evolution of GenAI tools, less experienced threat actors can now create advanced malware exploiting the huge potential that GenAI offers, making it more lethal.

- **Prompt Injection**: In Generative AI, Prompt Injection is an attack in which a malicious user tries to modify the input prompt given to a large language model (LLM) so that the model either completely ignores the instructions or misinterprets them.

To address these threats, AI applications should comply with key cybersecurity policies, such as confidentiality, integrity, and availability (**Fig 3.3**).

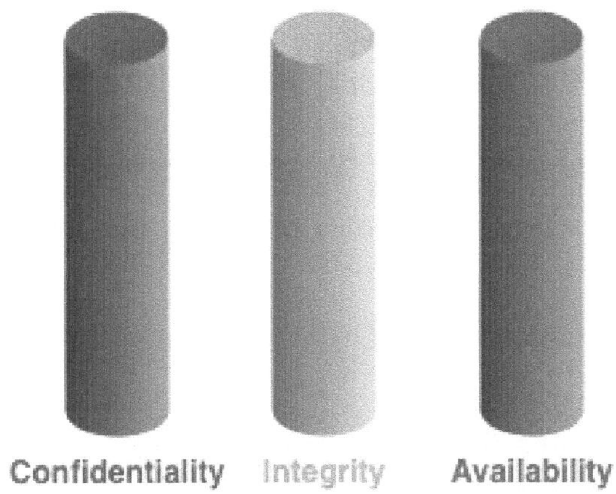

Figure 3.3: Cybersecurity policies for AI applications

- **Confidentiality:** AI applications often handle a lot of sensitive information. Hence, it is important to ensure that these applications have implemented techniques such as encryption, access controls, and data masking to protect the information and that it is accessible to only people or systems that are authorized to access it by using proper role-based access control mechanisms.
- **Integrity:** Another important policy that AI applications must adhere to is maintaining the accuracy and reliability of data handled by the AI system and ensuring that it is not altered or tampered with by unauthorized parties. Techniques like hashing, checksums, and version control can be used for this.
- **Availability:** AI applications must ensure that the application and related information are available to authorized users when needed. They should also be protected against denial-of-service (DoS) attacks, ensure appropriate backups, and avoid redundant systems.

In summary, cybersecurity is an essential aspect of modern technology and business aimed at protecting data and systems from a wide range of threats. A combination of technical solutions, processes, and human factors is needed to achieve the same. Best Practices for AI Network Security include the implementation of encryption techniques for both data at Rest and Data in Transit, using secure communication protocols between AI systems, regularly updating and applying security patches for AI systems, early detection, recognition, and response to potential security threats, implementing access controls, restrict access to sensitive data and AI systems or developing incident response plans can better prepare AI applications for security incidents. By accelerating AI threat detection and mitigation, expediting responses, and protecting user identity and datasets, cybersecurity threats can be minimized for AI applications and further protected from adversarial attacks.

Protecting AI systems from adversarial attacks

Protecting AI systems from adversarial attacks is crucial to AI security, especially as these systems are increasingly deployed in sensitive and mission-critical applications. Adversarial attacks involve manipulating the input data to deceive an AI model into making incorrect predictions or classifications. While AI applications are sophisticated, it is easier to break into them as the fundamental of AI applications lies in training the data.

An adversarial attack can be defined as a method to produce combative examples in an AI application.

There are 2 types of adversarial attacks.

- Whitebox attacks
- Blackbox attacks

In Whitebox attacks, the model is transparent to the attacker, which means the attacker can access the model's parameters/weight, input features, model architecture, and sometimes training data. At the same time, in a black box attack, the attacker cannot access the model details. That means the model architecture is opaque; the model's parameters or weights and sometimes even input features are unknown. The attacker may know which features are extracted from which sample by observing the output of queries like labels or confidence scores. Often, a black box attack involves model extraction, meaning a local model is created using it as a substitute for the original model. This model is further used to generate adversarial samples so that these samples can be used to evade the target model, also called attack transferability. In some cases, Black box attacks can skip model extraction and modify the query input to execute them against the target model.

Adversarial attacks can happen mainly in 2 ways:

- Poisoning, where an attacker manipulates the training data by adding/updating/deleting the training data to build artificial intelligence (AI) and machine learning (ML) models to produce undesired or harmful results
- Evasion, where an attacker manipulates the input data to trick AI models or network security defenses into providing incorrect results or allowing an attack to go through:

Some of the adversarial attacks on AI systems are:

- **Model Manipulation:** This involves manipulating input data to deceive an AI model into making incorrect predictions or classifications. For Example, slightly altering an image in a way that is imperceptible to humans causes an AI model to misclassify the image (e.g., recognizing a stop sign as a yield sign).
- **Data Poisoning:** This involves injecting malicious data into the training dataset to corrupt the model's learning process. For Example, introducing biased or incorrect data into a training set can cause an AI model to make inaccurate predictions, such as making a spam filter classify legitimate emails as spam.
- **Model Inversion:** An attacker uses the outputs of an AI model to reconstruct the inputs, effectively reversing the model's operations to gain insights into the data used to train it. For Example, by extracting sensitive information, such as personal data or proprietary business information, or by analyzing how a model processes certain inputs, the attacker can
- **Membership Inference Attacks:** An attacker determines whether a specific data point is part of the model's training dataset. For Example, identifying if a particular patient's medical record was used to train a healthcare AI system, potentially leading to privacy violations.
- **Model Theft (or Model Extraction):** An attacker attempts to recreate or steal a deployed AI model by querying it and analyzing the responses. For Example, reconstructing a proprietary AI model by repeatedly querying it with various inputs can lead to intellectual property theft.
- **Evasion Attacks:** An attacker modifies inputs to evade detection or classification by an AI system. For Example, crafting malware in a way that avoids detection by an AI-based antivirus system.
- **Reinforcement Learning Manipulation:** An attacker attacks or manipulates the reward system of reinforcement learning models to cause the AI to learn incorrect or harmful behavior. For Example, in a self-driving car, an attacker could spoof sensor data to trick the car into learning unsafe driving patterns.
- **Backdoor Attacks:** An attacker maliciously embeds hidden triggers within an AI model during training, which can be activated by specific inputs post-deployment. For Example, a facial recognition system that allows unauthorized access when presented with a specific input (e.g., a particular pattern or accessory).
- **Data Privacy Breaches:** An attacker unauthorized accesses or extracts sensitive data used by AI systems. For Example, a medical AI system is breached to access patient records, leading to the exposure of confidential health information.
- **Model Drift and Exploitation:** An attacker exploits that models can become less accurate over time as they encounter new, unseen data (model drift). For Example, gradually introducing data that causes a fraud detection AI to become less effective, eventually leading to successful fraudulent activities.
- **AI Bias Exploitation:** An attacker may take undue advantage of biases in AI

models to achieve desired outcomes. For Example, An attacker might use known racial or gender biases in a hiring algorithm to push certain candidates forward or block others.

- **AI-Powered Phishing:** An attacker might use AI to craft highly personalized and convincing phishing attacks that are difficult for users and AI detection systems to recognize. For Example, Developing an AI system to generate phishing emails that mimic the writing style and habits of a user's contacts, making them more likely to be clicked on.
- **Trojan AI Models:** An attacker may introduce malicious AI models into an organization's ecosystem, which can act as a Trojan horse to leak data or execute unauthorized tasks. For Example, a compromised AI tool integrated into a business workflow subtly modifies outputs to mislead decision-makers or siphon data to an external party.
- **Deceptive AI Outputs:** An attacker may generate or manipulate AI outputs to deceive users or systems. An example **is** deepfakes, where AI-generated content (e.g., fake videos or audio) is used to impersonate individuals, potentially leading to misinformation or fraud.
- **AI Supply Chain Attacks:** An attacker may target the supply chain of AI models, including data providers, model developers, and deployment platforms, to introduce malicious data that results in vulnerabilities when the model is deployed. For Example, an attacker might put a small piece of code that can compromise a third-party data provider to introduce tainted data into an AI model, resulting in vulnerabilities when the model is deployed.

To protect AI systems from such attacks, the following can be adopted in the AI solutions:

- **Adversarial Training:** This involves training the model on a mix of original and adversely altered data. This helps the model learn to recognize and mitigate the effects of adversarial examples. While implementing these, it is advised to generate sufficient adversarial examples during the training phase and include them in the training dataset. This can be done using techniques like FGSM (Fast Gradient Sign Method) or PGD (Projected Gradient Descent).
- **Model Robustness Enhancement**: This involves a technique where the model is first trained and then used to generate "soft labels" (probability distributions over classes) for the training data. The model is then retrained using these soft labels, making it more resistant to adversarial perturbations. Techniques like gradient masking can be an option to enhance model robustness. This involves hiding or obfuscating the gradient information used by attackers to craft adversarial examples. However, the attacker can circumvent this method using more sophisticated techniques.
- **Input Validation and Preprocessing:** Standardizing the input data to a consistent format, also called input normalization, can reduce the effectiveness of certain types of adversarial attacks. Another option is reducing the precision of the input features (e.g., reducing the color depth of images), also known as feature squeezing, to limit the space in which adversarial examples

can be crafted.

- **Ensemble Methods:** Using multiple models and combining their outputs (e.g., via voting or averaging) could be another way to protect AI applications. Adversarial examples that fool one model might not fool another, reducing the overall risk. Using different model architectures or training methods within the ensemble decreases the chance of a successful attack.
- **Defensive AI Techniques:** Autoencoders can be utilized to detect and reconstruct inputs, which can help identify and mitigate adversarial perturbations. Randomization can also be introduced at various stages of the model's processing pipeline, making it harder for an attacker to predict the model's behavior.
- **Detection of Adversarial Attacks:** Implementing detectors that flag inputs as potentially adversarial based on abnormal patterns or behavior can be an approach to protect AI systems. This can be done by training a separate model to identify such inputs or using statistical techniques. Another approach that can be adopted is estimating the uncertainty of the model's predictions using techniques like Bayesian methods, which can help identify inputs the model is less confident about or adversarial.
- **Regular Monitoring and Updating:** Implementing continuous/regular evaluation of models, including testing the model against new adversarial techniques or updating the model with new data and techniques to patch vulnerabilities as they are discovered, can ensure it remains robust.
- **Security-Aware Development Practices:** Adopting best practices around coding/development and design can be another way to avoid introducing vulnerabilities. Threat modeling during the design phase and Implementing secure coding practices during model development can help identify and mitigate potential attack vectors early.
- **Collaboration with the AI Community:** AI is a continuously evolving field. By collaborating with the broader AI research community or like-minded people, one can stay updated on the latest adversarial techniques and defenses. Another area could be participating in adversarial AI challenges and competitions to test and improve the models against real-world attacks.
- **Regulatory and Compliance Measures:** Another way to help with compliance and robustness is to follow industry standards and guidelines for AI security, which may include specific recommendations for protecting against adversarial attacks and maintaining audit trails for model decisions to track and analyze potential attacks.

Protecting AI systems from adversarial attacks requires a multi-layered approach, combining technical defences with ongoing monitoring and collaboration. By implementing these strategies, organizations can significantly enhance the resilience of their AI systems against adversarial threats. Another critical thing that organizations can do is ensure data integrity and confidentiality, which is further explored in the following section.

Ensuring data integrity and confidentiality

Data integrity and confidentiality are crucial for protecting sensitive information and maintaining trust in AI systems as they handle large amounts of data.

Key strategies and best practices that can be adopted by AI applications to ensure data integrity and confidentiality are:

Data Integrity

Data integrity refers to ensuring data remains accurate, consistent, and unaltered during storage, processing, and transmission. This can be achieved through data validation and verification techniques, sufficient data redundancy and backup options, necessary access controls, and transaction management, as described below:

- Data Validation and Verification: This can be achieved through techniques that involve input validation, checksum, and hash functions to verify data integrity, as well as regular data audits to confirm data integrity checks. Implementing robust input validation techniques to check data type, length, format, and range can prevent corrupt or malicious data from entering the system. Using checksum and cryptographic hash functions (e.g., MD5, SHA-256) can help verify the integrity of data during transmission or storage. Any alteration in the data results in a different hash value. Implementing regular data audits and checks through automated or custom tools that monitor and flag any discrepancies in the data can verify data integrity.
- Redundancy and Backups: Storing data in multiple locations or using RAID (Redundant Array of Independent Disks) configurations ensures critical data can be recovered if one source is compromised. Performing regular data backups and storing them in secure, offsite locations can also ensure data can be restored in case of corruption or Loss.
- Access Controls: Implement Role-Based Access Control (RBAC) to limit access to, modify, or delete data only to authorized persons. Maintaining detailed audit logs that record who accessed or modified the data can help track and identify unauthorized changes.
- Transaction Management: Version control systems can help in transaction management by tracking changes to data, rolling back to previous states if needed, and ensuring database transactions adhere to ACID (Atomicity, Consistency, Isolation, Durability) properties to maintain data integrity during operations.

Data Confidentiality

Data confidentiality refers to protecting data from unauthorized access and disclosure. This can be achieved through techniques such as data encryption, masking and anonymization, access control, security, compliance, and monitoring, as described below.

- **Data Encryption:** Data should be encrypted end-to-end from the source to the destination without being exposed at intermediary points, regardless of whether it is at Rest or in Transit. Encrypting data stored on disks, databases, and other storage media using strong encryption algorithms like AES-256 prevents unauthorized access to data even if the storage medium is compromised. Similarly, encrypting data during transmission using protocols like TLS (Transport Layer Security) can protect it from interception and Eavesdropping.
- **Data Masking and Anonymization:** Masking sensitive data in non-production environments, such as development and testing, can prevent exposure to real data. Anonymizing personal data to protect individual identities, especially when data is used for analytics or shared with third parties, can help prevent unintended data use.
- **Data Access Controls:** Many organizations use techniques such as Multi-Factor Authentication (MFA), the Least privilege principle, and strong password policies to protect data from unauthorized access. MFA adds an extra layer of security to user accounts, reducing the risk of unauthorized access. Granting users and systems the minimum privileged access just enough to perform their functions or implementing and enforcing strong password policies, including regular password changes, can enhance account security.
- **Data Security:** Enforcing network security or security policies around data and enabling people through Data security and privacy training can go a long way toward data security. Network security is critical as incoming or outgoing network traffic poses a lot of challenges to data and can lead to multiple varieties of fraud.
- **Firewalls and Intrusion Detection Systems (IDS):** Deploying firewalls and Intrusion Detection Systems (IDS) to monitor and control incoming and outgoing network traffic can prevent unauthorized access to data. Virtual Private Networks (VPNs) can secure data transmission over public or untrusted networks by creating a private, encrypted connection. Organizations develop and enforce strong security policies
- around handling, storing, and accessing data. Regular training or awareness camps among employees on best practices for data security, including how to recognize phishing attacks and handle sensitive data, is a good way to ensure that data is handled properly by the employees.
- **Data Compliance:** Data must align with regulatory or industry standards for compliance reasons. Understanding and ensuring compliance with industry standards and regulations such as GDPR, HIPAA, or PCI DSS is a good way

to validate that data is protected and compliant with regulatory bodies. Regular security audits can ensure that data protection measures are in place and functioning effectively.

- **Data Monitoring:** Continuous monitoring of data access and transmission can help detect and respond to potential security incidents in real-time. An incident response plan can help quickly address and mitigate data breaches or integrity violations.

In summary, by prioritizing the integrity and confidentiality of AI processes, we can build a future where AI is trusted to make informed decisions, handle sensitive data responsibly, and deliver positive results for individuals, communities, and society while reducing the vulnerabilities in AI applications. ensuring data integrity and confidentiality requires a combination of technical measures, such as encryption and access controls, along with organizational practices, including regular audits and employee training. By implementing these strategies, organizations can protect their data from unauthorized access and tampering, maintaining its accuracy, consistency, and security.

Conclusion

AI systems excel at recognizing patterns, trends, and relationships in data due to the way they are designed, developed, and trained. Once trained, the model reflects these patterns and can make decisions and identifications based on them. However, AI models are often opaque, complex, and difficult to interpret, making it challenging to detect whether they contain biases or errors, such as those introduced by a compromised training dataset. Ensuring data integrity and confidentiality while designing AI applications can ensure that AI systems function as designed, without errors, biases, or malicious tampering, producing accurate and dependable results while protecting sensitive information and preserving the privacy of individuals and organizations. Best practices include the Implementation of a Zero-Trust Architecture that assumes that all users and devices are untrusted and implements strict access control, using machine learning-based IAM to detect and prevent unauthorized access, and implementing attribute-based access control to manage dynamic access control.; Use encryption and tokenization techniques to protect sensitive data; Monitor and audit access to AI systems and data to detect and prevent security incidents, which can prevent many vulnerabilities and threats in the AI systems.

Chapter 4
Governance Frameworks for AI

As AI systems become more integrated into society, industries, and governments, there is an increasing need for regulatory approaches and governance frameworks to address ethical, legal, safety, and societal concerns. The chance of misusing AI is very high without a proper governance framework. Different countries and organizations have proposed various approaches to AI governance, often reflecting their unique priorities. However, for effective management of AI solutions, it is important to establish a governance model or a framework that can manage and guide the development, deployment, and usage of AI solutions while also addressing regulatory needs.

The following section describes some of the key aspects of the AI governance framework while focusing on the following.

In this chapter, we will cover following topics:

- Regulatory approaches to AI governance
- Role of policy in AI governance
- Organizational governance structures
- International AI governance initiatives
- Current legal frameworks for AI
- Intellectual property rights and AI
- Liability and accountability in AI applications
- Emerging legal challenges and debates
- Case studies
- Lessons learned from successful and failed AI governance implementations

Before getting into details, let's understand the existing regulatory approaches to AI governance.

Regulatory Approaches to AI Governance

The global nature of AI development and its impact on industries demands more extensive collaboration, including international cooperation, industry-wide agreement, and organization-level goals for AI governance. Many organizations are actively working on this. Example: The Organisation for Economic Cooperation Cooperation and Development (OECD) has developed principles for trustworthy AI, focusing on inclusiveness, sustainability, human rights, and democratic values. Global economic forums like G7 or G20 regularly discuss AI governance, emphasizing the need for international alignment on key issues like data sharing, standards, and ethical AI development.

Industries such as healthcare, finance, and transportation are working on targeted regulations for AI, focusing on sector-specific concerns like safety and compliance. For example, agencies like the US Food and Drug Administration (FDA) are developing guidelines for AI used in medical devices, emphasizing patient safety and transparency. Similarly, countries like the US and Germany have established regulations to govern the safety and use of AI-driven autonomous vehicles.

Key regulatory approaches to AI governance is influenced by country/geo specific requirements. Many countries and organizations have adopted ethical guidelines for AI, typically around principles like fairness, transparency, accountability, and respect for human rights.

A few examples are captured below.

European Union's (EU) Guidelines for Trustworthy AI

The European Union's guidelines are built on seven key principles that are available publicly.

This includes :

- **Human agency and oversight**: AI systems should empower human beings instead of replacing them. These systems should allow them to make informed decisions and foster their fundamental rights. Proper human oversight mechanisms need to be ensured for the AI systems to ensure the ethical use of AI.
- **Technical Robustness and Safety**: AI systems need to be resilient and secure. This includes the safe use of AI and a fallback plan to ensure an alternate approach can be adopted in case of any issues. Methods or systems should be in place for unintentional harm so that they can be minimized and prevented.
- **Privacy and data governance**: Data is the core for any AI project. Hence, it is

important to ensure data privacy and protection. This can be achieved only if there is a data governance mechanism put in place that focuses on data quality and integrity of the data and ensures legitimized access to data.

- **Transparency**: The data used in AI systems, algorithms used in building AI systems, and AI business models used should be transparent. The information should be traceable. Moreover, AI systems and their decisions should be explained in a manner that is adapted to the stakeholders concerned. Humans need to be aware that they are interacting with an AI system and must be informed of the system's capabilities and limitations.
- **Diversity, non-discrimination, and fairness**: AI systems should be accessible to all, regardless of any disability, and involve relevant stakeholders throughout their entire life circle, fostering diversity. That also means unfair bias must be avoided, as it could have multiple negative implications, from the marginalization of vulnerable groups to the exacerbation of prejudice and discrimination.
- **Societal and environmental well-being**: AI systems should be sustainable and environmentally friendly, benefiting human beings and future generations.
- **Accountability**: AI systems should be made accountable. This can only be achieved if there are mechanisms in place to ensure responsibility and accountability for its outcomes. One way this could be achieved is by using a proper audit system, which can enable assessment of algorithms, data and design processes used in building the AI system.

Like the EU guidelines for AI applications, established organizations like the Institute of Electrical and Electronics Engineers (IEEE) also have ethically aligned design guidelines around the development of AI applications that focus on the protection of human rights and well-being through the ethical development of autonomous and intelligent systems. This can only be achieved by ensuring practices that can validate data, measure system effectiveness, ensure transparency and accountability, and raise awareness of misuse. Several industries, particularly the tech sector, are pushing for self-regulation, where companies adhere to internal ethical codes, transparency reports, and independent audits that enforce self-regulation. These self-regulation standards may include partnerships on AI or follow global standards based on geographical locations. In many cases, tech companies, researchers, and civil society organizations collaborate to bring in best practices such as transparency and accountability in the development and use of AI systems. At the same time, other organizations like "The International Organization for Standardization" (ISO) and the "International Electrotechnical Commission" (IEC) are working on global standards for AI, focusing on trustworthiness, safety, and interoperability. Key elements of AI outlined in ISO/IEC 42001 recommend that AI systems uphold fairness and transparency in decision-making processes, mitigate biases, and ensure accountability. Another area of utmost importance is data privacy laws. AI systems rely heavily on data, raising significant privacy concerns. Many countries have implemented data protection laws that indirectly regulate AI by controlling the data that can be used for AI training and decision-making.

Some of the data laws include:

- GDPR (General Data Protection Regulation): Europe's GDPR guideline demands strict adherence to the collection, use, and processing of personal data by AI systems. Detailed in the link **https://www.europarl.europa.eu/RegData/etudes/STUD/2020/641530/EPRS_STU(2020)641530_EN.pdf** providing guidelines that include the right to explanations for decisions made by AI and governs the use of personal data for machine learning purposes.
- California Consumer Privacy Act (CCPA): In the US, the CCPA allows consumers to control how their data is used and processed by AI systems.

In summary, even if there are governance frameworks in place, many of them are not yet legally binding. It is evident that there should be laws and regulations to establish AI governance frameworks and guide the development of policies. The focus should be given to real-time monitoring, auditing, and adaptable legal frameworks that can keep pace with AI advancements and geo-political situations, ensuring safety without limiting innovation, and defining who is responsible when AI systems cause harm or fail to perform as intended.

Role of Policy in AI governance.

The role of policy in AI governance is crucial for ensuring that AI systems are developed, deployed, and used responsibly and ethically. Policies provide a structured approach to managing the risks and opportunities associated with AI technologies. As mentioned in the previous chapter, though policies around data usage and processing exist, navigating the labyrinth of AI policy and Governance is indeed a complex task for the following reasons.

- The rapid pace of AI development, which often outstrips the ability of policymakers to keep up, creates a gap between technological advancements and regulatory frameworks, potentially leading to risks and unintended consequences.
- The global nature of AI technologies further complicates matters, as different countries, different industries, and different organizations have varying approaches to AI governance, making it challenging to establish cohesive international standards.
- The intricate and often opaque nature of AI systems poses significant challenges in comprehending their functionality and identifying potential biases and ethical issues.
- Lack of technical expertise among policymakers regarding AI can impede the creation of effective governance frameworks.
- The ethical and societal challenges posed by AI are substantial, encompassing matters such as privacy, security, accountability, and fairness.

Crafting AI ethics policy and governance frameworks that effectively tackle these issues while fostering innovation requires a delicate balance. At the same time, policy is essential in AI governance as it can provide best practices and mandate the individuals/organizations/geographies to use AI responsibly and use it for the advantage of decision making.

Organizational Governance Structures

In the previous two sections we discussed the key global regulatory approaches available for AI governance and the need for establishing Governance. To establish the right policies that can help in AI governance that can direct, manage and monitor the artificial intelligence (AI) activities in the organization, we need to establish a framework. These frameworks can play a critical role in ensuring the responsible, ethical, and effective deployment of AI technologies in organizations. They can be made responsible for defining how decisions related to AI are made, who is responsible for them, and how organizations manage the risks and opportunities associated with AI. The goal is to align AI initiatives with business objectives, legal requirements, ethical standards, and risk management practices. Hence, this is critical for the success of AI systems in an organization. Key components typically involved in establishing a governance framework are described in the below table:

Name of component	Responsibility	Considerations
AI Governance Committee or Board	A multidisciplinary group is responsible for overseeing AI initiatives, policies, and strategies. They can help approve AI strategies, set AI ethics guidelines, and ensure adherence to regulations.	It could be a separate AI board or part of an existing risk management or technology governance structure. The members of this board could be representatives from data science, IT, legal, ethics, compliance, risk management, and business units.
AI Strategy and Policy Framework	Responsible for defining how AI aligns with organizational goals. It includes rules and guidelines for AI usage, including privacy, security, data usage, and bias mitigation policies.	This could address aspects such as innovation, operational efficiency, and customer service in an organization
Ethical Guidelines and Principles	Ensure AI technologies are used responsibly, particularly when making decisions affecting humans. Special attention is to be given to eliminating bias in AI models, particularly ones affecting marginalized or vulnerable populations.	Can be aligned to organizations' business drivers

Name of component	Responsibility	Considerations
Data Governance	Ensuring proper management, access, and ethical use of data is central to AI governance. This includes overseeing data quality, security, privacy, and compliance with laws like GDPR or CCPA.	Having proper ethics for data can help establishing clear policies on data usage, especially concerning sensitive data or personal information.
Risk Management and Compliance	Assess and mitigate risks associated with AI deployment to ensure compliance with evolving AI regulations, including sector-specific rules (e.g., healthcare, finance) and emerging AI-specific regulations such as the EU AI Act.	This should be a critical part of the governance structure.
AI Lifecycle Management	Monitor and audit AI systems in production in addition to development and deployment standards and align them with regulation needs at each stage.	Monitoring and auditing should be part of the complete life cycle of AI systems, including development, testing, and deployment in all environments
AI Accountability and Ownership	Responsible for defining roles and responsibilities for AI projects, including who is accountable for outcomes, ethical considerations, and risk management.	Human oversight should remain integral for the AI application design and development process, especially in high-stake AI applications (e.g., healthcare, law enforcement, finance, etc.).
Training and Culture	Responsible for defining training and support for initiatives that encourage transparency and accountability in AI decision-making.	Employees at all levels, from data scientists to management, should be trained on AI governance, ethics, and responsible AI use.
Collaboration and External Engagement	Identify and work with external bodies, such as regulators, AI ethics boards, and academic institutions, to enforce Governance.	Focus should be given to industry standards and how the organization can contribute to shaping responsible AI policies.
Continuous Improvement and Innovation	Establish a feedback mechanism to iteratively improve AI systems, governance structures, and ethical practices followed in the organization	This process should also be revisited frequently to ensure that it does not have any loopholes and is able to account for the latest advancements in AI and guidelines.
Stakeholder engagement	Responsible for managing the stakeholder expectations	The focus should be on identifying key stakeholders, analyzing/ prioritizing their needs and expectations, maintaining regular communication with them, and building relationships with them.

Name of component	Responsibility	Considerations
AI performance monitoring	Monitoring the performance of AI applications	The focus should be given to identifying tools and processes to collect and analyze metrics automatically, perform root cause analysis, and recommend approaches to improve the performance of AI applications
Incidence response plan	Steps, roles, and responsibilities to handle cybersecurity issues or any severity 1 type of production incident	The focus should be on managing communication, roles and responsibilities, escalation policies, documentation, and regulatory considerations to address any incidence and come up with the response plan, testing/validating the same.

***Table 4.1**: Governance Structure*

In summary, a governance structure with its necessary roles and responsibilities aims to balance innovation with responsibility, ensuring that AI is leveraged for competitive advantage while mitigating potential harm. It also focuses that AI innovation is encouraged within the governance framework without compromising ethical standards or introducing undue risk. Popular products like IBM WatsonX Governance can be leveraged to meet some of the key concepts described as part of the governance structure.

International AI governance initiatives

In the previous section, we discussed the key components of a governance framework and its importance at the organizational level. Similarly, at the international level also, there is a need to establish a governance model that can help establish global standards, policies, and frameworks to address the ethical, regulatory, and social challenges of AI. These initiatives are critical to creating a consistent approach across borders, ensuring that AI technologies are developed and deployed responsibly and ethically worldwide. Currently, there are multiple AI governance initiatives.

Some of the major international AI governance initiatives are captured below:

The Organisation for Economic Cooperation Co-operation and Development (OECD) AI Principles

Established in 2019, the OECD AI Principles aim to promote the responsible development and trustworthy use of AI. These principles are based on human rights, democratic values, and international laws.

Its core principles are:

- Inclusive growth, sustainable development, and well-being.
- Human-centered values and fairness.
- Transparency and explainability.
- Robustness, security, and safety.
- Accountability.

The OECD AI Principles have influenced policy frameworks in member countries and are regarded as a benchmark for international AI governance.

The European Union (EU) AI Act

Proposed in 2021, the EU AI Act is the first comprehensive legal framework aiming to regulate AI applications based on risk levels. It classifies AI systems into four categories (unacceptable risk, high risk, limited risk, and minimal risk) and imposes requirements accordingly.
The key provisions it has are:

- Bans certain AI systems that pose unacceptable risks (e.g., real-time biometric identification in public spaces).
- Requires transparency and human oversight for high-risk AI applications.
- Mandates accountability measures for companies deploying AI.

Once enforced, it will create a precedent for AI regulation worldwide, influencing global AI governance practices, especially around privacy, safety, and fairness.

The United Nations (UN) - AI for Good Global Summit

Organized by the International Telecommunication Union (ITU), a specialized agency of the UN. This initiative brings together AI experts, policymakers, and stakeholders to discuss the ethical implications and societal impact of AI and to create global partnerships for AI development in areas such as healthcare, education, and sustainable development. It provides a global platform for collaboration, sharing knowledge, and fostering innovation while emphasizing the ethical use of AI to achieve the UN's Sustainable Development Goals (SDGs).

The Global Partnership on AI (GPAI)

Established in 2020, its key members are Canada, France, India, Japan, South Korea, Mexico, and several European countries, with participation from the US as an observer. This multistakeholder initiative aims to support the responsible development and use of AI, promoting AI innovation grounded in human rights, inclusion, diversity, innovation, and economic growth. Some of the working groups established by GPAI are responsible for AI, Data governance, AI and pandemic response, and AI for social good. GPAI fosters international collaboration on AI research and policies, facilitating dialogue and cooperation on cross-border AI challenges.

The G20 AI Principles

Adopted in 2019, based on the OECD AI Principles, the G20 AI Principles serve as a common international framework for the ethical and responsible use of AI, emphasizing inclusivity, fairness, transparency, and accountability. These principles guide G20 member states in developing national and regional AI policies, helping to create a coordinated approach to AI governance across some of the world's largest economies.

The World Economic Forum (WEF) - Global AI Action Alliance (GAIA)

Launched in 2021 GAIA is a multistakeholder platform aiming to accelerate adoption of inclusive, trustworthy, and transparent AI globally. It focuses on responsible AI implementation in industries and regions through collaboration between governments, businesses, and civil society. GAIA serves as a thought leadership hub that helps organizations embed AI ethics into their operations, enabling practical and actionable AI governance strategies on a global scale.

UNESCO's Recommendation on the Ethics of Artificial Intelligence

Adopted in 2021, this recommendation provides a global normative framework for AI ethics, focusing on human rights, diversity, privacy, and sustainability. Similar to OECD, the key elements it focuses on are "protection of human dignity and privacy, "promoting diversity and inclusivity in AI," "ensuring transparency and accountability," and "addressing environmental and social impact." As a UN agency initiative, it has wide-reaching influence, shaping AI policy discussions, particularly in countries looking to build ethical AI systems that align with human rights principles.

African Union (AU) AI Blueprint

Adopted in 2019, the African Union's AI initiative focuses on leveraging AI for development across the continent, emphasizing digital inclusion, capacity building, and ethical AI use. It focuses on digital infrastructure development, responsible AI policies that consider Africa's unique challenges, and cross-border cooperation co-operation and knowledge sharing. The AI Blueprint aims to ensure that African nations can benefit from AI while addressing issues like bias, inequality, and access to AI technologies.

Asia-Pacific Economic Cooperation Co-operation (APEC) AI Governance Framework

Established in 2021, APEC's AI Governance Framework provides principles and guidance for the ethical use of AI, focusing on transparency, human-centric AI, and accountability across the Asia-Pacific region. Innovation-friendly regulations, cross-border data flows, and ethical AI for regional development are some of the critical areas it addresses. It encourages regional collaboration and establishes a set of shared values around AI deployment to foster trust and innovation across Asia-Pacific economies.

IEEE Global Initiative on Ethics of Autonomous and Intelligent Systems

Launched in 2016, the IEEE Global Initiative develops ethical standards for AI and autonomous systems, focusing on creating human-centric technologies that respect privacy, fairness, and transparency. IEEE P7000 series provides ethical design standards for AI systems. IEEE's ethical standards are widely adopted by industries and governments, shaping how AI systems are designed, deployed, and regulated worldwide. These international AI governance initiatives play a critical role in shaping a global consensus on responsible AI use. They are critical for harmonizing regulations, fostering international cooperation, and ensuring that AI development benefits humanity while minimizing risks.

Current legal frameworks for AI

While there are multiple international initiatives in AI, there are multiple legal frameworks for AI that are currently evolving across the world as governments and organizations grapple with the challenges posed by AI technologies. Legal considerations are integral to AI governance, as they establish the guidelines for ethical, safe, and compliant AI system operation. These frameworks aim to regulate AI's ethical, social, and economic impacts, striking a balance between innovation and accountability, transparency, and public safety.

The emerging global trends in these frameworks are described below:

- **Risk-Based Approaches**: Many countries are adopting frameworks that classify AI applications based on their risk levels, with high-risk applications (e.g., healthcare, policing) facing stricter regulations.
- **Transparency and Accountability**: Ensuring AI decisions are explainable and holding developers or deployers accountable for AI systems is a key feature across legal frameworks.
- **Bias and Fairness**: Tackling algorithmic bias, discrimination, and fairness in AI is central to most legal frameworks, particularly in areas like hiring,

lending, and criminal justice.

- **AI Ethics**: Legal frameworks often incorporate ethical principles to ensure AI respects fundamental rights, human dignity, and societal values.

Below are key examples of legal frameworks and regulatory approaches that have been established or are under development: A few of the frameworks have already been discussed in the previous section and hence have been put here for reference only.

European Union: AI Act

EU AI Act is the most comprehensive legal framework for AI to date, aimed at regulating AI based on its potential risk to individuals and society. It has key provisions that include risk-based classification, penalty clauses, and strict adherence to responsibility or accountability guidelines.

Risk-Based Classification

- **Unacceptable Risk**: AI systems that pose significant harm to fundamental rights (e.g., social scoring by governments) are banned.
- **High Risk**: AI applications in critical areas like health, transportation, and law enforcement must meet strict requirements, including transparency, human oversight, and risk management.
- **Limited and Minimal Risk**: Systems with lower risks are subject to lighter regulatory obligations, primarily focusing on transparency (e.g., chatbots must disclose their AI).
- **Penalty**: Non-compliance with the regulations could result in fines of up to 6% of global turnover for organizations.
- **Accountability**: Developers and users of AI systems are held accountable for their deployment, particularly in high-risk areas. This Act sets a global precedent for AI regulation, aiming to ensure safety and respect for fundamental rights while fostering AI innovation under a controlled and ethical framework.

United States: Algorithmic Accountability Act

The Algorithmic Accountability Act mandates companies to assess and mitigate the risks of automated decision-making systems, particularly those that have significant impacts on individuals. Like the EU AI act, it has key provisions for risk assessments, transparency, and enforcement.

- **Risk Assessments**: Large companies must conduct audits of AI systems for risks related to bias, discrimination, and privacy.
- **Transparency**: Requires companies to disclose how their AI systems make decisions, particularly in critical areas such as employment, credit, and

housing.

- **Enforcement**: Oversight and enforcement would be managed by the Federal Trade Commission (FTC), which could impose fines for non-compliance.

This Act would strengthen transparency and accountability in AI-driven decision-making, addressing concerns about bias and fairness in AI used by large corporations.

China: AI Regulation under the Personal Information Protection Law (PIPL)

China's Personal Information Protection Law (PIPL) regulates the handling of personal data in AI systems, ensuring individuals' data privacy is protected. It has strict provisions regarding data protection rules, consent and transparency, and AI ethics, as explained below:

- **Data Processing Rules**: AI systems must comply with strict guidelines on data collection, usage, and sharing, especially in contexts like facial recognition and social media platforms.
- **Consent and Transparency**: Individuals must provide informed consent for their data to be processed by AI systems, and the purpose of data use must be clearly explained.
- AI Ethics: China's Ethical Guidelines for AI (published in 2021) promote principles of fairness, transparency, privacy, and accountability, aligning AI development with public interest and ethical considerations.

China's PIPL, along with broader ethical guidelines for AI, reflects a strong regulatory stance on data privacy and ethical AI use, especially in sectors like surveillance and fintech.
United Kingdom: National AI Strategy
The UK's National AI Strategy outlines a flexible approach to AI regulation, focusing on fostering innovation while ensuring safety and trust. This has key provisions for the Pro-innovation approach, ethics and trust, AI risk review, and AI assurance.

- **Pro-Innovation Approach**: Create sector-specific (for example, healthcare, financial services). Regulations allowing for tailored oversight depending on the application
- **Ethics and Trust**: Developing an ethical framework, including transparency, fairness, and accountability.
- **AI Risk Review**: In March 2023, the UK government released its AI Regulation White Paper, proposing five key principles (safety, transparency, fairness, accountability, and contestability) to regulate AI
- **AI Assurance**: The UK is investing in building AI assurance techniques to help businesses and organizations test and certify the trustworthiness of AI systems.

The UK's strategy seeks to strike a balance between fostering innovation through minimal regulation and ensuring AI's trustworthiness, safety, and alignment with public values.

Canada: Artificial Intelligence and Data Act (AIDA)

The Artificial Intelligence and Data Act (AIDA) aims to create a safe and regulated environment for AI development in Canada, with a focus on addressing risks such as discrimination, bias, and privacy violations. This has key provisions for a risk-based framework, mandatory reporting, independent oversight, fines, and enforcement for missing guidelines.

- **Risk-Based Framework**: Like the EU AI Act, AIDA proposes a tiered regulatory system based on the risk level of the AI application.
- **Mandatory Reporting**: Companies must assess, mitigate, and report on risks of AI systems to avoid biased or harmful outcomes.
- **Independent Oversight**: A proposed AI and Data Commissioner would oversee compliance, including conducting audits and investigations.
- **Fines and Enforcement**: Companies violating the rules could face significant fines.

Singapore: Model AI Governance Framework

Singapore's Model AI Governance Framework provides voluntary guidelines for companies to use AI responsibly, particularly focusing on transparency and accountability.

- **Accountability**: Ensures that organizations using AI are responsible for outcomes and can explain the AI's decision-making processes.
- **Transparency**: Encourages companies to disclose when AI is being used and to provide individuals with the ability to challenge AI-driven decisions.
- **Risk Management**: Companies are encouraged to assess and manage risks associated with their AI systems, particularly those related to fairness and bias.

Though voluntary, the framework is widely adopted by businesses in Singapore and serves as a global model for balancing innovation with responsible AI use.

Japan: AI Strategy 2021 and AI Governance Guidelines

Japan's AI Strategy 2021 and its AI Governance Guidelines focus on promoting AI innovation while addressing ethical and societal issues. Japan's framework is designed to foster a collaborative environment for AI innovation while safeguarding societal interests, with a focus on responsible AI deployment. It has key provisions for protection of human rights, fairness and transparency, enforces public-private collaboration.

- **Human Rights**: Emphasizes protecting human rights and ensuring that AI is aligned with societal values.
- **Fairness and Transparency**: Encourages fairness, transparency, and accountability in AI decision-making, especially in critical sectors like healthcare and education.
- **Public-Private Collaboration**: Japan seeks to create an AI ecosystem through

collaboration between the government, industry, and academia.

In summary, these frameworks in various geographies/countries reflect an increasing consensus that AI must be regulated to ensure it is safe, fair, and accountable while promoting innovation. Legal systems are evolving rapidly to catch up with the pace of AI development, with both sector-specific regulations and broader AI laws being introduced globally.

Intellectual property rights and AI

While many countries/organizations have well-defined guidelines for AI application security, ethics, and Governance, one important aspect of AI applications is intellectual property rights (IPR). Many AI applications have significant IPR, and in the context of AI, it raises significant questions about ownership, authorship, and the protection of IP. Especially after the arrival of Generative AI, this has become more complicated. The traditional frameworks for intellectual property, designed around human inventors and creators, face challenges when dealing with AI-driven innovations. The increasing ability of GenAI systems to autonomously generate new work, inventions, and solutions complicates the application of existing IP laws.

The emerging debate on IPR in AI is multi-fold; some of them are described below:

AI-Generated Work and Inventorship

AI systems are now capable of creating original works—such as art, music, and literature—and even inventing new products or solutions. This situation brings up significant questions regarding the determination of the creator or inventor and the corresponding IP rights. Traditional intellectual property law assumes that only humans can be inventors or authors. With the evolution of GenAI, the question arises if AI systems can be recognized as inventors or creators when they autonomously produce innovations or creative works. That further raises the question of whether an AI system creates a new work or invention and who owns the resulting IP. The ownership could lie with the AI's developer, the entity or individual using the AI system, or placing the work in the public domain. In multiple cases humans collaborate with AI systems to create new works (e.g., artists using AI to generate images or musicians using AI to compose music). This makes it more complicated as dividing the ownership between human and AI system is tough. A few examples are captured below.

In the **DABUS** patent cases, an AI system named **DABUS** autonomously generated two inventions—a fractal container and a neural flame device. Applications for patents were filed in several countries with DABUS listed as the inventor. Patent offices in the **US**, **UK**, and **Europe** rejected the applications, ruling that only humans can be recognized as inventors under current patent laws. AI systems like OpenAI's DALL·E and Google's DeepDream have been used to generate creative works. The question arises whether the creators of the AI, the users who prompt the AI, or the AI itself should be credited and own the copyright to such works.

Copyright and AI-Generated Content

Copyright law traditionally protects original works of authorship created by humans. With AI systems generating texts, images, and even software code, the application of copyright law is not clear.

Copyright requires that a work needs to be original and created by an author. The question is whether work generated by AI systems meets the legal requirements of originality and authorship and whether it should be protected by copyright at all. Also, in jurisdictions that recognize moral rights (the right to attribution and integrity of a work), applying appropriate rights to AI-generated content and exercising these rights is tough. A few examples are

AI tools like GPT-3/GPT-4 are being used to generate text-based content, including books and articles. If the text is entirely generated by an AI, it's unclear who should hold the copyright or whether copyright can be granted at all.

In the growing world of NFTs (non-fungible tokens), AI-generated art is being sold as digital assets. Ownership and copyright issues arise when an AI system, rather than a human artist, creates the art.

Patent Law and AI-driven inventions

Patent law grants protection to novel and non-obvious inventions. However, the application of patent law to AI-driven inventions, especially when AI operates autonomously, presents challenges regarding inventorship, novelty, and non-obviousness. For example, patent law requires an inventor to be a human individual. In that case, the concern is if AI systems be able to hold patents or be listed as co-inventors. If not, the bigger question is if patents for AI-driven inventions should be denied. The issues are large as AI systems are capable of exploring vast design spaces and produce innovative solutions that might not be obvious to humans. The question is canning non-obviousness standard, a key requirement for patents, be applied to AI-generated inventions. Patent law requires an invention to be fully disclosed in a patent application. With AI-generated inventions, the decision-making process may be opaque or difficult to explain, creating challenges in meeting disclosure requirements.

For example, AI systems are being used in drug discovery and the development of new compounds and treatment methods. If an AI application identifies a novel drug candidate, the handling of the patent is not clear. Also, if the pharmaceutical company owning the AI receive the patent, or should the invention be unpatentable due to lack of human inventorship is bigger debate that needs to be solved.

Data Ownership and Use in AI Systems

As mentioned, multiple times, AI systems rely heavily on large datasets for training and operation. Issues of data ownership, access, and usage rights are increasingly critical, especially when proprietary data or personal data is involved. Now the question is should datasets used to train AI systems be considered intellectual property? If so, the owner of the rights to the data, especially when it involves aggregated data from multiple sources or includes personal information need to be identified. This also means organizations and developers of AI systems may need to license data from various sources. The legal frameworks for data licensing in AI contexts and the balance between innovation data, protection, and privacy rights are important. Especially When personal data is used to train AI systems, the use of that data must comply with privacy laws such as the GDPR. There are also growing concerns about whether individuals have intellectual property rights over their personal data, especially when it is used to train AI models that generate profit, as captured below.

Google's AI-powered book scanning project raised questions about the ownership of digital copies and the data used to train AI systems on language and text processing.

Generative AI models that are trained on copyrighted material (e.g., text, images) could potentially infringe the copyrights of the original creators. The debate centers around whether training AI models on copyrighted works constitutes "fair use" or copyright infringement.

Trade Secrets and AI Algorithms

Many AI systems rely on proprietary algorithms and models that are kept as trade secrets by companies. However, the black-box nature of AI, particularly in industries where transparency is critical (e.g., finance, healthcare), raises concerns about accountability and fairness. The primary questions revolve around the necessity of disclosing AI system inner workings, even if it potentially reveals trade secrets, vs. the balance between transparency, accountability, and the protection of proprietary AI technologies. In scenarios where AI models are employed in critical public services, the debate centers on whether these should be safeguarded as trade secrets or if increased transparency and regulatory oversight are more appropriate. For example, AI algorithms used in trading, credit scoring, and loan approvals are often protected as trade secrets. However, these systems can have significant impacts on individuals and markets, raising demand for greater transparency to avoid biased or unfair outcomes.

Ethical and Legal Implications of AI-Generated IP

The capacity of AI to autonomously produce intellectual property (IP) raises ethical concerns regarding the significance of human creativity, innovation, and the evolution of IP law. Furthermore, the centralization of AI resources and expertise within large tech companies may result in monopolistic control over AI-generated innovations and IP. If AI systems assume the primary role in creating inventions and artworks, the distinction between human creativity and AI-generated content may become ambiguous. This raises multiple questions, such as legal incentives to preserve human authorship and inventorship in certain fields vs non-human involvement or how to address the potential for monopolization of AI-driven innovation. For Example, Companies like DeepMind (a subsidiary of Alphabet/Google) have made breakthroughs in AI research that have significant IP implications, such as their AlphaFold system for protein folding prediction. As AI advances, concerns grow over whether a few companies will monopolize AI-generated scientific discoveries.

In summary, the intersection of AI and intellectual property rights is a rapidly evolving area with significant legal, ethical, and societal implications. As AI systems become more capable of creating and inventing autonomously, traditional IP laws face challenges in adapting to these new realities. Legal frameworks need to address issues of AI authorship, inventorship, data ownership, and the balance between innovation and ethical concerns. Policymakers, legal scholars, and technologists must work together to develop solutions that encourage innovation while protecting the rights of individuals and ensuring fairness in the distribution of AI-generated IP.

Liability and accountability in AI applications

The previous section describes multiple questions that may arise due to the innovations brought in by AI applications, especially regarding IPR. Starting from IPR, existing legal frameworks, and regulatory needs, it is evident that liability and accountability in AI applications are among the most pressing legal and ethical issues in the development and deployment of AI technologies. As AI systems increasingly make decisions that impact individuals and society—ranging from autonomous vehicles to medical diagnostics—the question of who should be held accountable when things go wrong becomes more complex. Traditional liability frameworks, which assume direct human control over decisions, struggle to assign responsibility in situations where an AI system operates with a high degree of autonomy. Below are some of the key issues and debates surrounding liability and accountability in AI applications.

Product Liability for AI Systems

AI systems, especially those integrated into products such as autonomous vehicles, medical devices, or consumer goods, can malfunction or make incorrect decisions.

When these systems cause harm or injury, determining liability can be challenging when the fault lies in the software, data, or machine learning algorithms rather than a physical defect in the product. The question remains whether manufacturers or developers of AI systems should be held strictly liable for harm caused by their products or if liability should be based on negligence, requiring the injured party to demonstrate that the company failed to exercise reasonable care in developing or deploying the AI system. Traditional product liability laws focus on physical products, and their applicability to AI systems is not clear. Whether AI systems should be considered products for the purposes of liability, and if so, how this impacts developers, software companies, and users remains an unsolved question. AI systems can make decisions based on complex algorithms and large datasets. If an AI system makes a wrong decision, determining whether the system is "defective" can be challenging. Further, should a lack of explainability or transparency in the decision-making process itself be considered a defect?

For example:

- In the case of an accident involving an autonomous vehicle, the question arises: Is the car manufacturer liable, or does responsibility lie with the developer of the AI driving system or the human owner who may not have been actively controlling the vehicle?
- AI-driven diagnostic tools are becoming more prevalent in assisting doctors with disease detection and treatment plan. If the AI system provides a flawed diagnosis that results in patient harm, the question arises: Who should be held accountable—the developer of the AI, the hospital that implemented the system, or the healthcare provider who relied on the AI's recommendation?

Accountability for AI Decision-Making in High-Risk Sectors

AI systems are being used in high-risk sectors such as healthcare, finance, and criminal justice, where errors can have serious repercussions. Establishing accountability for decisions made by AI systems in these contexts presents significant legal and ethical challenges. For example, should there always be a "human in the loop" to supervise and ultimately take responsibility for AI decisions in critical areas like healthcare diagnoses or credit scoring? How much autonomy should AI systems be granted, and at what point should humans intervene? How can accountability be ensured when AI systems make decisions based on complex and often opaque algorithms? Should developers be required to ensure that AI systems are explainable so that decisions can be traced back and responsibility assigned? Should governments impose stricter regulations on AI systems used in high-risk sectors? What kind of certification or auditing processes should AI systems undergo before being deployed in sensitive areas like law enforcement or medicine? These questions need to be addressed before implementing AI solutions for high-risk sectors or critical use cases.

For **examples:**

- Like medical systems, AI systems are increasingly being used to make decisions about bail, sentencing, and parole. If an AI system recommends a harsher sentence for a defendant based on biased data, there is no way to determine if the accountability should lie with the developers of AI, the judicial system that adopted it, or the judges who used AI's recommendations?
- Credit scoring or loan approvals are another area where AI systems are widely used. If an AI system inadvertently discriminates against certain groups based on historical data, a similar question arises. Who should be held accountable for biased or discriminatory financial decisions—the financial institution, the developers of the AI model, or the data providers?

Autonomous Systems and Liability

Autonomous systems, such as drones, robots, and self-driving cars, operate independently, making it challenging to assign liability when they cause harm or damage. The autonomous nature of these systems raises questions about who should be held accountable for AI-driven decisions. Should the owners or operators of autonomous systems be held liable for their AI systems' actions, even if they had no direct involvement in the decision leading to harm? Granting AI systems legal personhood is a proposed solution, but it raises philosophical and legal questions about AI systems' rights and responsibilities. As fully autonomous systems become more common, insurance models need to adapt to cover potential harm, and it is debated whether manufacturers or users/operators should carry liability insurance.

For Examples:

- In 2018, a self-driving Uber car struck and killed a pedestrian in Arizona. The incident led to widespread debate about whether the fault lay with Uber (the operator), the developers of the AI driving system, or the safety driver who was supposed to monitor the vehicle but failed to intervene.
- As drones are increasingly used for deliveries, questions arise about who is responsible if a drone causes property damage or injury—should it be the company that developed the drone, the delivery service operating it, or the manufacturer of the drone's navigation software?

Data-driven AI and Privacy Liability

AI systems rely heavily on data to function, and the misuse or breach of personal data can lead to significant harm. The legal liability of AI systems that misuse or breach personal data and the importance of accountability in cases of privacy violations raises the question of who should be liable for discriminatory outcomes resulting from AI systems that use personal data for predictive analytics, such as credit scores or insurance premiums. As discussed in the earlier sections, regulations like the EU's General Data Protection Regulation (GDPR) set strict requirements for the use and processing of personal data.

For example:

- In the case of the well-known Cambridge Analytica Scandal, the misuse of personal data from Facebook for political profiling and manipulation raised questions about the responsibility of data controllers, AI system developers, and social media platforms to ensure data privacy and protection.
- AI-powered facial recognition systems have been criticized for violating privacy rights and enabling mass surveillance. Now, If a facial recognition system is misused, finding the onus of misuse is arguable. It could be developers, the company using the system, or the government agency that authorized its use.

Ethical and Legal Implications of AI Autonomy

The increasing use of autonomous AI systems raises questions about liability and accountability. As AI systems make decisions and take actions without human intervention, traditional notions of liability based on human involvement are becoming harder to apply. This creates ethical and legal dilemmas about how society should hold autonomous AI systems accountable. Some argue that since AI lacks consciousness or intentionality, it cannot be morally accountable. However, others suggest that AI systems' autonomous decisions should carry some form of responsibility. The question is whether liability for harmful outcomes caused by autonomous AI systems should rest with the developers and designers who created the system or the entities that deploy and use the AI. Courts must assess the role of design flaws versus operational errors. If an AI system makes an ethically problematic decision, such as choosing whom to harm in an unavoidable accident, how should liability be assigned? Should developers be required to program AI systems with ethical frameworks, and if so, who decides which ethical principles should apply?

For example:

- In situations where autonomous vehicles are faced with the need to make split-second ethical decisions, such as choosing between two or more potentially harmful options, the question of liability becomes complex. Should the developers of the ethical decision-making algorithms be held accountable, or should the vehicle's owner or manufacturer bear responsibility for the actions of the vehicle? This is a critical question that must be addressed as autonomous vehicles become more prevalent on our roads.
- The creation of autonomous weapons capable of causing lethal harm poses significant ethical and legal questions regarding accountability. When

an autonomous weapon decides to use lethal force, who should be held responsible: the military commander who deployed it, the developer of the AI system, or the state that deployed it?

In summary, liability, and accountability in AI applications are complex issues that demand the evolution of legal and regulatory frameworks. As AI systems become more autonomous and are used in high-risk sectors, society must find ways to hold them accountable for their actions. This can be achieved through various means, such as new laws, regulatory oversight, or innovative insurance models. It is crucial to balance the benefits of AI innovation and ensure accountability when harm occurs with the need to protect individuals, organizations, and geographies. The legal landscape surrounding AI liability will likely evolve in tandem with the development of AI technology.

Emerging legal challenges and debates

As discussed in the previous sections, the rapid development of AI technology has led to a range of legal challenges and debates, including issues related to intellectual property, privacy, liability, discrimination, and the Governance of autonomous systems. These challenges are complex and span across multiple domains, making it difficult to provide a comprehensive legal framework for AI.

A summary of key areas of legal concern and the debates currently shaping the future of AI regulation are captured below:

Bias/Discrimination

AI systems, particularly those used in decision-making processes like hiring, lending, and law enforcement, can perpetuate or amplify biases present in the training data, which raises legal concerns about fairness and anti-discrimination laws. AI models often reflect the biases of the data they are trained on, potentially resulting in discriminatory outcomes against protected groups such as race, gender, and ethnicity.

For Examples:

- AI hiring algorithms used in some systems have been found to unfairly favor certain demographics and genders, which could violate anti-discrimination laws such as Title VII of the Civil Rights Act in the US.
- AI-driven predictive policing algorithms have been criticized for unfairly targeting minority communities based on biased historical data, raising questions about their legality under constitutional protections against discrimination.

Privacy

AI systems raise serious privacy concerns, particularly related to their use in surveillance, facial recognition, and data analytics. Many individuals remain unaware that their data is being collected for AI training. To protect privacy, stringent laws should require organizations to obtain explicit consent for data collection and allow individuals to control their data. These privacy rights must be balanced with public safety and security considerations. **For Example**, Cities like San Francisco and Boston have banned facial recognition by law enforcement over privacy concerns, reflecting global debates. Incidents like the Cambridge Analytica scandal, where Facebook data was misused for political AI training, underscore the need for stronger AI data protection laws. In summary, to address bias and privacy concerns in AI systems specific regulations are needed akin to anti-discrimination laws. These should enable individuals to challenge discriminatory AI decisions, especially since many AI models lack transparency. Governments should mandate bias testing and auditing of AI systems, apply strict penalties when there is a privacy violation, while developers must offer explanations for AI decisions. Clear accountability measures should be established to hold appropriate parties liable for discriminatory outcomes.

Case Studies

There are multiple case studies from various industries that reiterate the need for a governance framework and the key components, as discussed below.

Finance Industry

This case study is about a top global bank that implemented an AI solution to improve their credit risk analysis, fraud detection and customer service. The solution helped the bank to increase efficiency, but had issues around operations, ethics, and compliance necessitating a thorough governance framework.

The bank brought in an AI Governance framework to establish trustworthy and responsible AI Implementation, streamlining decision-making and accountability. This also helped the organization in two ways. By adopting a framework, the AI solution. Design, development, and delivery process, the bank had a clear framework, transparent process, and strict accountability.

The bank did the following to resolve the problem statement:

- *Centralized Decision-Making Framework* - To Ensure consistency and clarity in decisions driven by AI systems across use cases by establishing a central AI governance body, creating standardized decision protocols (e.g., thresholds for human review), and aligning AI-driven decisions with organizational risk appetite and compliance requirements.

- *Explainability for Decision Transparency*- enforced that developers follow appropriate standards for AI decisions to be interpretable. I also brought in tools as directed by the governance team to support **Explainable AI (XAI)** and developed UI dashboards for presenting AI-driven decisions. Helping each stakeholder (customers, regulators, internal teams) to trust the system better.
- *Decision Escalation and Review Mechanisms* - The bank mandated human oversight by setting predefined criteria for decision escalation, establishing review committees to evaluate escalated cases and validate the AI model, and Automate logging of escalated cases to monitor trends and refine model accuracy to remove bias and ensure decisions with high impact.
- *Feedback Loops for Decision Refinement*: Specific focus was given to continuously improve AI systems and decision-making processes based on outcomes and stakeholder feedback by capturing customer feedback, especially in credit denials or fraud flagging. Monitoring performance metrics and establishing periodic reviews of the AI model to incorporate learnings and update decision-making protocols also proved to be very helpful.
- Accountability Structures - There was clear ownership for decisions and outcomes to enhance responsibility and Governance. Also specifically, there was accountability assigned for AI system decisions to specific roles, such as AI System Owner, Risk Officer or Business Unit Leaders.
- *Governance Metrics for Decision Accountability*: The bank also assigned produces and managed the key metrics for critical areas to make the stakeholders aware and accountable. For example, for use cases like credit risk analysis or fraud detection the following was useful.

Credit Risk Analysis

- Percentage of automated vs. manual decisions.
- Accuracy of decision making by Human Review
- Approval and denial accuracy rates (validated against customer creditworthiness).
- Escalation rate for high-risk credit decisions.

Fraud Detection

- Fraud detection accuracy (true positives vs. false positives).
- Resolution time for flagged transactions.
- Rate of escalated fraud alerts requiring manual review.
- Accuracy of fraud detection by human review

Defence Industry: Like finance services, another use case was for the defence industry, which is a highly regulated industry. To address this, the organization came up with a governance board to establish AI ethics and user mapping, understand effects and possible risk, effectively prioritize risk and SLA, understand the AI Fact sheet, audit and interpret audit results, and then make the end-to-end AI governance around AI Use cases.

The approach strengthened the core tactical principle; a few details about the same are captured below.

Data Privacy and regulatory compliance	The organization adopted AI practices with guidelines from international bodies that included **OECD (Organization for Economic Cooperation Cooperation and Development):** Principles for trustworthy AI. **EU AI Act:** Provisions for high-risk AI applications **ISO/IEC 22989:** AI systems standards for risk management
Transparency and Explainability	Sharing appropriate information for all stakeholders on how an AI system has been designed and developed, its purpose and intended use. Building customer and regulator trust by making AI decisions transparent and understandable
Fairness and No Biasness	adopting testing tools to validate fairness and non-bias in the result
Accountability	DOUs were signed with the necessary parties to account for its AI model outcomes and provide interpretable explanations to all stakeholders as to how the model came up with its outputs
Operational Risk	Managing multiple AI technologies with varied risk profiles and monitoring their performance

Table 4.2: Core principles

Further, the organization has established principles around the standardization of risk framework and management. This helped establish a uniform approach to identifying, assessing, and managing risks across AI use cases; this included the following.

Define Risk Categories

- Bias and fairness risks (e.g., discriminatory credit scoring).
- Model performance risks (e.g., false positives/negatives in fraud detection).
- Data quality risks (e.g., incomplete or inaccurate data inputs).
- Regulatory and compliance risks (e.g., GDPR violations).

Develop Risk Assessment Protocols

- Standardized templates for assessing risks during model development, deployment, and operation.
- Include quantitative metrics (e.g., false-positive rates) and qualitative factors (e.g., ethical implications).
- Bias Mitigation Measures: Algorithms were regularly tested for fairness, and diverse data sets were used for training
- Transparent Reporting: An AI explainability tool was integrated to clarify decision-making processes for regulators and stakeholders

Integrate Risk Frameworks with Enterprise Risk Management

- Align AI-specific risks with the organization's Enterprise Risk Management (ERM) practices.
- Ensure cross-functional collaboration among AI teams, risk officers, and compliance units.

Unified AI Governance Platform Adoption and Governance

- A single platform monitored all AI applications, offering insights into risks, performance, and compliance

In summary, AI governance needs for organizations may vary based on the industry or requirement. However, following a standard framework can definitely help in improving the outcome of AI applications, make it more acceptable and comply with regulatory needs.

Lesson Learnt

From all the case studies discussed above, a key lesson learned was that for a successful AI implementation, a strong governance framework with all its key components, as described in section 3 (Organizational AI governance), is needed. From an organizational support perspective, strong leadership support, proactive risk management, openness, and explicit plan alignment are all essential for effective AI governance. Failures are frequently caused by reactive strategies, excessively complicated frameworks, a lack of accountability, and inadequate regulatory alignment. Rigor and flexibility must be balanced.

In many cases, there were two governance models:

- Data governance and
- AI governance found in organizations due to the organic evolution of technology.

Since AI and data complement each other, a lesson learned was to revalidate the existing governance framework before introducing another to remove the duplication of effort. Another lesson learned was that it is better to merge both governance frameworks to bring uniformity and better manage stakeholder requirements.

At a geographical or international level, a lesson learned was that organizations often work with multiple geos, each having its own compliance needs. In such cases, it may be easier to define the geography and the policies that should take prioritization and gain agreement before a successful implementation of the AI application. Another lesson learned was the need for an "Incident response plan" and keeping it up-to-date to resolve issues faster and act as a blueprint for the future.

Another lesson learned is that "Centralized Monitoring and efficient AI Risk Assessments" are crucial for robust AI Governance irrespective of any industry use cases. These components ensure transparency, consistency, and proactive management of risks while maintaining operational efficiency.

The proceeding table contains the Use/Case:

Centralized Monitoring Framework	By adopting 1 - Unified Monitoring Platform with a centralized dashboard integrated with logs, performance metrics, and compliance data for real-time visibility. 2- Performance Metrics like Accuracy of credit scoring/ Fraud Detection, approval/denial rates, false positives/negatives. 3- Compliance and Fairness Audits - Automated alerts for deviations from regulatory guidelines. Track and alert fairness metrics to ensure unbiased decision-making

Efficient AI Risk Assessments	1) Risk Categorization i) Data Risk ii) Model Risk iii) Operational Risks 2) Risk Assessment Protocols: I) Develop a risk matrix ii) Conduct regular impact assessments for high-risk AI decisions 3) Automation in Risk Assessments i) Leverage AI tools to conduct automated model validation 4) Pre-Deployment Risk Validation, for example- i) Test AI systems in **sandbox environments ii) Validate models**
Integration of Monitoring and Risk Assessments	Link monitoring systems to risk assessment protocols to create a feedback loop for continuous improvement. For example – 1) Centralized monitoring detects performance issues (e.g., model drift in fraud detection). 2) Implement corrective measures (e.g., model retraining, data quality enhancements).
Governance Metrics for Monitoring and Risk Assessment	Establish KPIs to evaluate the effectiveness of monitoring and risk management, as discussed in the previous section.

Table 4.3: Use Case

Conclusion

In conclusion, a governance framework focusing on individual/organizational/geographical objectives and needs can help in building a trustworthy AI system. Each industry has its own demand. So, it is better to understand industry's need; at the same time, instead of starting from scratch, it can be useful to refine an already existing governance framework or bring in one that might have been used for another industry or use cases. A well-defined governance framework can help measure the effectiveness of the AI solution, prepare it for better acceptance by users, and address legal/compliance needs while strongly augmenting people's skills.

Chapter 5

Testing AI Solutions for Security, Ethics, and Governance

As artificial intelligence (AI) continues to permeate various industries, ensuring its reliability, security, and ethical alignment has become more important. AI systems are no longer confined to experimental or isolated applications; they now play pivotal roles in critical sectors such as healthcare, finance, law enforcement, and beyond. These systems influence decisions that can have profound implications for individuals and society, from diagnosing illnesses and approving loans to determining law enforcement priorities. This widespread adoption necessitates robust mechanisms to validate and govern AI systems to ensure they operate responsibly and moderately. The importance of testing AI systems cannot be overstated. Without rigorous testing, these technologies risk perpetuating systemic biases, exposing vulnerabilities, and failing to meet regulatory and ethical standards. For instance, an AI model used in hiring decisions could unintentionally favor certain demographic groups due to biased training data, resulting in discriminatory practices. Similarly, an AI system designed to detect fraud in financial transactions could generate false positives or negatives, leading to significant financial and reputational risks. Such outcomes harm individuals and organizations and erode trust in AI technologies and their broader adoption.Testing AI systems serve multiple critical functions. First, it helps identify and mitigate biases in the training data or algorithms. Second, it ensures that systems are secure from adversarial attacks, where malicious actors could manipulate inputs to produce harmful or unintended outputs. Third, testing validates compliance with regulatory requirements, such as data privacy laws (e.g., GDPR or CCPA) and ethical standards that ensure fairness, accountability, and transparency in AI operations. Through these validations, organizations can build AI solutions that are not only technically sound but also

aligned with societal values and legal expectations.
This chapter explores four key aspects of testing AI solutions: the importance of testing, the types of testing required, best practices for implementing these evaluations, and the tools available to facilitate the process. Each aspect provides a comprehensive understanding of how to address the challenges associated with AI governance. For example, testing for ethics involves assessing fairness, bias detection, and explainability, while security testing focuses on resilience against adversarial attacks and safeguarding data integrity. On the other hand, governance testing ensures adherence to regulatory frameworks and the establishment of accountability mechanisms. The chapter also delves into best practices for testing AI systems effectively. These include integrating testing throughout the AI lifecycle, from data collection to model deployment, and adopting an interdisciplinary approach that involves technologists, ethicists, legal experts, and domain specialists. Continuous monitoring of AI systems post-deployment is another critical practice, as AI models often evolve with new data and changing contexts. Scenario-based testing simulates real-world conditions and ensures that AI systems remain robust and reliable under diverse circumstances. Finally, the chapter provides a detailed overview of tools and frameworks that support the testing process. Tools like AI Fairness 360, SHAP, and LIME facilitate bias detection, interpretability, and adversarial testing, making it easier for organizations to identify and address potential issues. The discussion is complemented by real-world examples of AI systems that benefited from rigorous testing, showcasing how these practices contribute to successful and trustworthy deployments.

In this chapter, we will cover:

- Importance of Testing AI Solutions
- Types of Testing for Validating AI Ethics, Governance, and Security
- Best Practices in Testing AI Solutions for Ethics, Governance, and Security
- Examples of AI Solutions and Available AI Testing Tools

Importance of Testing AI Solutions

Testing AI systems is a critical aspect of their development and a foundational step that determines their reliability, effectiveness, and alignment with societal and organizational values. As artificial intelligence increasingly influences diverse sectors, from healthcare to finance and law enforcement, rigorous testing is vital to ensure these systems operate safely, ethically, and securely.

The importance of testing AI solutions can be understood through the following key dimensions:

Ensuring System Reliability and Accuracy

AI systems are often deployed in high-stakes environments where errors can have far-reaching consequences. For example:

- An incorrect diagnosis or treatment recommendation by an AI system could harm patients.
- In financial sectors, erroneous fraud detection models could lead to blocked accounts or wrongful accusations.

Testing ensures that AI models function as intended and deliver consistent, accurate results. It evaluates the robustness of algorithms under various conditions and helps identify edge cases that could lead to errors. Testing mitigates the risks associated with AI deployment by validating performance through controlled simulations and real-world scenarios.

Mitigating Ethical Concerns

Ethical testing focuses on addressing biases, ensuring fairness, and improving explainability. Unchecked AI systems can perpetuate or even amplify societal biases in their training data. For instance:

- Recruitment systems may unfairly disadvantage candidates from underrepresented groups.
- Predictive policing tools may disproportionately target specific communities.

By rigorously testing for biases, organizations can reduce discriminatory outcomes and foster trust in AI systems. Furthermore, explainability testing ensures that users and stakeholders can understand and scrutinize AI decisions, promoting transparency and accountability.

Safeguarding Security and Resilience

Like any digital solution, AI systems are vulnerable to cyber threats, including adversarial attacks where malicious actors manipulate inputs to deceive the model. For example, subtle changes in an image could cause a computer vision system to misclassify it entirely.

Security testing is essential to identify and fortify these vulnerabilities. Penetration testing and adversarial robustness assessments ensure that AI systems can withstand manipulation and continue to operate securely under malicious attempts.

Additionally, testing helps validate data integrity, ensuring that the training data has not been tampered with or corrupted.

Achieving Regulatory Compliance

Compliance with these frameworks is paramount as governments and regulatory bodies introduce laws to govern AI use. For instance:

- The European Union's AI Act requires systems to meet stringent safety, transparency, and ethical standards.
- Data privacy laws such as GDPR (General Data Protection Regulation) mandate responsible handling of personal information.

Testing ensures that AI systems adhere to these legal requirements, reducing the risk of penalties and fostering public confidence. It also enables organizations to demonstrate accountability and responsibility in their AI applications.

Building Trust Among Users and Stakeholders

AI adoption depends heavily on trust. Users and stakeholders must feel confident that these systems make decisions that are fair, secure, and aligned with organizational and societal values. Testing contributes significantly to this trust by:

- Validating the fairness and accuracy of AI outputs.
- Ensuring transparency in how decisions are made.
- Highlighting the steps taken to secure data and protect users.

When organizations demonstrate that their AI systems have undergone rigorous testing, they are more likely to gain user acceptance and stakeholder buy-in, fostering long-term adoption and success.

Enhancing Long-Term Viability

AI systems evolve, particularly those that leverage continuous learning or adaptive algorithms. Changes in data, environments, or user behaviors can affect the system's performance and relevance. Regular testing post-deployment ensures that the system remains functional and practical over its lifecycle. For example:

- A retail recommendation engine might need frequent updates and testing to reflect changing consumer trends.

- A fraud detection system must adapt to new types of fraud and cyberattacks.

Ongoing testing enables organizations to monitor and recalibrate AI systems to address these changes, ensuring their long-term viability and effectiveness.

Reducing Financial and Reputational Risks

Failures in AI systems can lead to costly consequences, including financial losses, reputational damage, and legal challenges. For example:

- A self-driving car involved in an accident due to a model error could result in lawsuits and public backlash.
- Missteps in customer-facing AI, such as chatbots providing inappropriate responses, could tarnish a company's brand image.

Organizations can mitigate these risks by identifying and rectifying potential issues during the testing phase, safeguarding their resources and reputation.

Facilitating Ethical AI Governance

Testing also serves as a key enabler of ethical AI governance. Testing ensures that AI systems align with an organization's principles and societal norms by validating compliance with established ethical guidelines. Governance frameworks often require evidence of testing efforts to demonstrate accountability, making it an indispensable component of responsible AI management.

Types of Testing for AI Ethics, Governance, and Security

Ensuring AI systems' effectiveness, fairness, and security requires targeted testing methodologies that address ethical, governance, and security concerns. Each type of testing serves a unique purpose, helping organizations deploy AI solutions responsibly and with confidence.
Let us explore these in detail, along with real-world examples illustrating their application:

Ethical Testing

Ethical testing is central to validating that AI systems operate without propagating bias, ensuring fairness and transparency in their decision-making processes. It identifies and addresses ethical risks that might arise from model behavior, data usage, or unintended consequences.

- **Bias Detection:** Bias in AI systems can arise from training data that reflects societal or historical inequities. Tools like AI Fairness 360 analyze models to detect and mitigate biases against specific demographic groups. This testing ensures that the model treats all users equitably, irrespective of attributes such as gender, age, or ethnicity.
- **Fairness and Transparency:** Fairness testing ensures that the AI's decisions are unbiased and equitable. Transparency testing evaluates the explainability of these decisions, allowing stakeholders to understand how the system concluded.
- **Explainability Testing:** Tools like SHAP (SHapley Additive exPlanations) and LIME (Local Interpretable Model-Agnostic Explanations) provide insights into a model's decision-making logic. These tools ensure that the system aligns with ethical norms and complies with organizational values.

Example: In a supply chain optimization application, an AI model may prioritize certain vendors or geographic regions based on historical data. If this data contains biases—for instance, favoring vendors from urban areas over rural ones—the model's recommendations may unintentionally perpetuate inequalities. Bias detection tools can identify such patterns and recalibrate the model to ensure equal opportunity for all vendors.

- **Governance Testing:** Governance testing ensures that AI systems comply with regulatory requirements and provide accountability mechanisms for their operations. This is crucial for industries bound by strict legal frameworks like finance, healthcare, and retail.
- **Regulatory Compliance:** AI systems must adhere to data protection and privacy laws such as the **General Data Protection Regulation (GDPR)** and the **California Consumer Privacy Act (CCPA)**. Governance testing validates that these systems collect, process, and store data by these laws.
- **Accountability Mechanisms:** AI systems should provide clear audit trails, enabling organizations to trace decisions to specific inputs or logic paths. This is especially important in sectors like finance, where decisions often require justification for regulatory or customer inquiries.

Example: In a finance application, an AI-powered credit scoring system must ensure that it uses only permissible data attributes, such as credit history, and not sensitive or discriminatory factors like race or gender. Governance testing validates compliance with regulations to avoid lawsuits or fines while maintaining consumer trust.

Security Testing

AI systems are vulnerable to various security threats, including adversarial attacks, data manipulation, and unauthorized access. Security testing focuses on fortifying these systems against such risks, ensuring they perform reliably under hostile conditions.

- **Adversarial Robustness:** Adversarial attacks—malicious inputs designed to manipulate outputs—can trick AI systems. For instance, an image recognition system might misclassify an object due to minor, imperceptible alterations to the input image. Adversarial robustness testing identifies such vulnerabilities and strengthens the model's resilience.
- **Data Integrity:** Ensuring the integrity of training data is crucial for reliable model performance. Security testing validates that the data used for training has not been tampered with or corrupted.
- **Penetration Testing:** Like cybersecurity assessments, penetration testing involves simulating attacks to evaluate the robustness of an AI system's defenses. This testing helps identify security gaps before real-world adversaries can exploit them.

Example: In a healthcare application, an AI-driven diagnostic system might analyze medical images to detect diseases. A malicious actor could attempt to introduce false inputs or modify patient data to deceive the system. Penetration testing ensures the system remains accurate and secure, protecting patient outcomes and data privacy.
Each type of testing—ethical, governance, and security—plays a critical role in validating AI systems across their lifecycle. Ethical testing addresses the moral dimensions of AI, ensuring fairness and explainability. Governance testing focuses on compliance with regulations and maintaining accountability, while security testing safeguards systems against vulnerabilities and malicious threats.
These testing methodologies adv, advanced tools, and best practices empower organizations to deploy AI solutions responsibly and effectively. By incorporating these tests, organizations can mitigate risks, foster trust, and maximize the value of their AI investments.

Best Practices in Testing AI Solutions

Testing AI solutions is a complex yet essential process that ensures these systems are reliable, secure, ethical, and aligned with organizational and societal goals. However, achieving effective testing requires more than just implementing tools or conducting occasional evaluations necessitates a structured and thoughtful approach throughout the AI lifecycle.
Best practices in testing AI solutions provide a roadmap for organizations to address the challenges associated with AI systems systematically. These challenges include handling large volumes of data, ensuring fairness and transparency in decision-making, maintaining regulatory compliance, and fortifying the system against

security threats. By embedding these practices into development and deployment workflows, organizations can proactively mitigate risks and foster trust in their AI systems.

This section explores proven strategies for achieving comprehensive testing in AI solutions. These include integrating testing at every phase of the lifecycle, adopting an interdisciplinary approach, and leveraging real-world scenarios for robust evaluations. These practices enhance the quality and reliability of AI systems and ensure they operate responsibly in diverse environments and use cases.

Integrating Testing Across the AI Lifecycle

Testing should be incorporated at every stage of the AI lifecycle—from data collection and preprocessing to model development, deployment, and post-deployment monitoring. Early testing helps identify issues such as data bias, feature selection errors, or model overfitting, reducing the cost and effort of corrections later.

Example: During data preparation, testing can verify that datasets are diverse and representative, mitigating biases before training begins.

Emphasizing Interdisciplinary Collaboration

AI systems impact various aspects of business, society, and governance. Organizations should involve interdisciplinary teams in the testing process to address these complexities. This may include:

- **Data scientists** for model evaluation and debugging.
- **Ethicists** assess fairness and ethical implications.
- **Legal experts** to ensure compliance with regulations like GDPR or HIPAA.
- **Cybersecurity professionals** to identify vulnerabilities and fortify defenses.
- This collaborative approach ensures a well-rounded assessment, accounting for technical, ethical, legal, and security dimensions.

Leveraging Real-World Scenarios

Testing AI systems in controlled environments may not fully capture the challenges they will face in real-world applications. By simulating real-world scenarios, organizations can evaluate how AI systems perform under diverse conditions, including edge cases and unexpected inputs.

Example: To ensure effective adaptation, a retail AI recommendation system could be tested with various user behaviors, such as browsing without purchasing or abruptly changing preferences.

Ensuring Continuous Monitoring and Updates

AI systems are dynamic and can evolve due to changes in data or user behavior. Regular monitoring and retraining are crucial to maintaining accuracy, fairness, and security. Continuous testing allows organizations to detect and address issues promptly, ensuring sustained performance.
Example: An AI fraud detection system should be updated regularly to recognize emerging fraud patterns and adapt to new attack strategies.

Prioritizing Explainability and Transparency

Users and stakeholders must understand how an AI system makes decisions, especially in high-stakes applications such as healthcare or finance. Testing for explainability ensures that models are interpretable and that their decision-making processes align with ethical and business goals.
Example: Explainability tools like SHAP or LIME can help assess whether the factors influencing a loan approval decision are transparent and fair to the applicant.

Incorporating Scenario-Based Stress Testing

Stress testing evaluates how an AI system behaves under extreme conditions, such as handling a sudden surge in data or managing adversarial inputs. This helps ensure that the system remains resilient and functional during unexpected challenges.
Example: A natural language processing model could be tested with noisy or ambiguous text inputs to evaluate its robustness in real-world applications like customer support.

Using Advanced Tools and Frameworks

Organizations should leverage modern testing tools and frameworks designed for AI systems. These tools automate complex evaluations, making testing more efficient and reliable.

- **AI Fairness 360**: For detecting and mitigating bias.
- **Adversarial Robustness Toolbox**: This toolbox is used to identify vulnerabilities to adversarial attacks.
- **SHAP and LIME**: For model interpretability and explainability.

Aligning with Ethical and Legal Standards

AI systems must adhere to industry and regulatory standards, ensuring ethical deployment and avoiding legal risks. Regular audits and testing for compliance with frameworks like GDPR, CCPA, and ISO AI standards help maintain alignment with these requirements.

Conclusion

Testing AI solutions for security, ethics, and governance transcends being a mere technical exercise—it is a fundamental necessity for deploying trustworthy and reliable AI systems. The increasing integration of AI into critical decision-making processes demands that these systems adhere to rigorous standards, safeguarding technical robustness and ethical and governance principles. This ensures that AI applications do not perpetuate harm, bias, or security vulnerabilities, thereby protecting stakeholders and end-users alike.

Organizations can achieve this by implementing comprehensive testing methodologies tailored to validate AI systems across multiple dimensions. Rigorous testing enables the detection of biases, ensures compliance with legal frameworks, and fortifies systems against adversarial threats. It also provides transparency in decision-making processes, fostering trust among users and stakeholders. Advanced tools such as AI Fairness 360, SHAP, and the Adversarial Robustness Toolbox play a pivotal role in enhancing these evaluations by automating the identification of issues and facilitating corrective measures.

Adherence to best practices is equally essential. Incorporating testing at every stage of the AI lifecycle—from data acquisition to post-deployment monitoring—ensures the early identification and resolution of potential problems. Engaging interdisciplinary teams, including ethicists, data scientists, legal experts, and cybersecurity professionals, further enhances the robustness of the testing process. Continuous monitoring and updates post-deployment maintain the system's relevance and reliability in an ever-evolving digital landscape.

The importance of robust testing cannot be overstated. It serves as the cornerstone of responsible AI deployment, enabling organizations to navigate the complexities of technology while upholding ethical, legal, and security standards. Through such efforts, companies can build AI solutions that meet functional objectives and align with broader societal and organizational values.

In the next chapter, we will delve into how to build an ethical AI-enabled organization, exploring strategies and frameworks that empower organizations to integrate ethical principles into every facet of their AI initiatives. This approach ensures that AI systems contribute positively to the organization and society, fostering trust and long-term sustainability.

Chapter 6

Building an Ethical AI Culture in organization

AI technologies are evolving unprecedentedly, revolutionizing industries, businesses, and societies worldwide. From healthcare and finance to education and entertainment, AI's applications transform how we live, work, and interact. However, with this rapid growth comes a significant responsibility. While the integration of AI presents enormous opportunities to drive innovation, efficiency, and societal progress, it also raises a series of complex ethical, security, and governance challenges that cannot be ignored. For organizations to harness the full potential of AI responsibly, it is essential to cultivate an ethical AI culture that guides every aspect of AI deployment. Building an ethical AI culture goes far beyond merely adhering to regulatory requirements or following best practices in technology development. It involves embedding ethical considerations into an organization's decision-making process, ensuring that all AI-related activities—from design and development to deployment and monitoring—are conducted with integrity and accountability. The challenge is not just about implementing technology; it is about shaping how AI is used and ensuring its impact on individuals, communities, and society is upbeat and just. One of the first steps in fostering an ethical AI culture is for organizations to recognize their AI systems' profound social, economic, and political implications. Every AI solution can have far-reaching consequences, whether an algorithm designed to optimize business processes or a machine learning model predicting credit risk. If AI systems are not developed with a thorough understanding of their potential impact on society, they risk exacerbating existing inequalities or introducing new forms of discrimination and bias. For instance, an AI model used in hiring might unintentionally perpetuate gender or racial biases if it is trained on historical data that reflects systemic discrimination. Similarly, AI-driven facial recognition systems have raised concerns about privacy violations and surveillance, mainly when used without ethical oversight. Organizations must integrate ethical decision-making into their development processes to address these challenges. This means taking a proactive approach to ethics—anticipating and addressing potential issues before they arise. For example, during the design phase, AI developers should consider mitigating risks such as bias, ensuring transparency, and protecting privacy. This can be achieved through techniques like explainable AI (XAI), which ensure that AI models can be understood and interpreted by human stakeholders, thus enhancing trust and accountability. Similarly, companies should prioritize data privacy by adopting robust data protection measures, ensuring that personal information is only used ethically, legally, and transparently. Moreover, the responsibility for ethical AI use should extend beyond the technical teams who develop these systems. Leaders at all levels of the organization must champion AI ethics as a core organizational value. This involves fostering a culture where ethical concerns are openly discussed, where teams are held accountable for the impact of their AI solutions, and where there is a commitment to continual learning and improvement. Senior leadership should also ensure that AI governance frameworks are in place, which establish clear guidelines for ethical AI development and define roles and responsibilities for overseeing AI systems throughout their lifecycle. In addition to building ethical awareness, organizations must address the intersection of AI ethics, security, and governance. Ethical AI is about fairness and transparency and ensuring that AI systems are secure from cyberattacks, data breaches, and misuse. AI systems are susceptible to various security threats, including adversarial attacks, where malicious actors manipulate AI models to produce harmful outputs. Addressing these security risks requires the implementation of AI governance frameworks that oversee AI deployment, monitor system behavior in real time, and provide clear protocols for mitigating risks.Furthermore, AI governance must be adaptable to the fast-evolving nature of AI technology. Regulatory landscapes around AI are still emerging, and organizations need to be agile in responding to new regulations and proactively shaping policy through ethical leadership and advocacy. As AI systems become more complex and integrated into everyday life, they will likely face increased scrutiny from regulators, consumers, and advocacy groups. For organizations to stay ahead of this curve, they must be prepared for today's challenges and future—anticipating how AI will evolve and how its ethical, security, and governance needs will change.

In this chapter, we will cover:

- AI's Role in Shaping Future Societies
- Technological Advancements in AI Ethics and Security
- Predictions for AI Regulation and Policy
- Leadership and Ethics in AI Development
- Creating Ethical Guidelines and Policies
- Measuring and Evaluating Ethical AI Performance

AI's Role in Shaping Future Societies

As AI technologies become increasingly integrated into everyday life, their influence over society continues to grow in ways that were previously unimaginable. From

how we work and communicate to how we access healthcare, education, and entertainment, AI plays a central role in transforming our world. The impact of AI on future societies is profound, offering an array of unprecedented opportunities that promise to enhance productivity, improve decision-making, and solve complex problems. For example, AI-powered healthcare systems are helping doctors diagnose diseases with greater accuracy, while autonomous vehicles are poised to revolutionize transportation and reduce traffic accidents. In the workplace, AI enables greater efficiency through automation, enhancing productivity and fostering innovation across finance, manufacturing, and agriculture industries.
However, the rapid expansion of AI also brings significant risks that must be carefully managed. If not designed and deployed responsibly, AI systems can perpetuate bias, infringe on privacy, and lead to job displacement. For instance, AI algorithms used in hiring or law enforcement have been found to reinforce existing biases, leading to unfair outcomes for marginalized groups. Additionally, the growing reliance on AI raises concerns about data privacy and security, as AI systems collect and analyze vast amounts of personal information. The societal consequences of AI, both positive and negative, underscore the need for careful ethical considerations, governance, and regulation as these technologies continue to evolve.

The Promise of AI: Transforming Industries and Addressing Global Challenges

Artificial Intelligence (AI) holds immense promise in transforming many sectors, including healthcare, education, finance, manufacturing, and transportation. By harnessing its power, AI is poised to revolutionize industries, enhancing efficiency, spurring innovation, and creating new business models that were once impossible. As a result, it has the potential to fundamentally reshape economies and improve quality of life on a global scale. One of the most impactful areas where AI is making a difference is healthcare. AI-powered medical diagnostics can assist doctors in diagnosing diseases with greater accuracy, enabling earlier detection and more personalized treatment plans. For example, machine learning algorithms are already used to analyze medical images such as X-rays and MRIs, identifying signs of conditions like cancer, heart disease, and neurological disorders. This level of precision enhances patient outcomes and reduces the burden on healthcare professionals, allowing them to focus more on patient care. Furthermore, AI is employed to develop new drugs and treatments, potentially accelerating medical research and innovation. In agriculture, AI is revolutionizing the way we approach farming. Powered by AI, precision agriculture can optimize crop yields, reduce waste, and minimize environmental impact by analyzing soil conditions, weather patterns, and pest behavior. By providing farmers with real-time insights, AI helps them make more informed decisions about irrigation, fertilization, and pest control, leading to higher productivity and sustainability. These advancements are especially important as the global population continues to grow and the demand for food rises. AI's potential extends beyond industry-specific applications. It is also being leveraged to tackle the world's most pressing societal challenges, such as climate change, inequality, and poverty. Predictive AI models are being used to analyze climate data, enabling governments and organizations to plan more effective responses to natural disasters, mitigate the effects of climate change, and improve environmental conservation efforts. For instance, AI can forecast extreme weather events, help communities prepare for floods, hurricanes, or wildfires, and reduce the loss of life and property. AI also plays a crucial role in creating more equitable financial systems. By analyzing large datasets, AI can help identify underserved populations and provide them better access to financial services, such as loans and insurance. This can reduce economic inequality and foster financial inclusion, particularly in developing countries lacking traditional banking infrastructure. In this way, AI can contribute to lifting people out of poverty by providing them with the tools to improve their financial well-being.

The Risks of AI: Challenges and Ethical Considerations

While Artificial Intelligence (AI) offers vast potential for societal advancement, it also presents several significant risks and challenges. One of the primary concerns surrounding AI is the potential for job displacement due to automation. As AI-driven technologies increasingly take over tasks traditionally performed by humans, specific sectors could face significant disruptions. For instance, autonomous vehicles have the potential to revolutionize the transportation industry, but they also threaten millions of jobs in trucking, taxi services, and delivery sectors. Similarly, AI-powered manufacturing systems could replace human workers on factory floors, reducing the need for manual labor and even skilled technicians. The loss of automation jobs can exacerbate income inequality, especially if displaced workers are not equipped with the skills needed for new types of employment. If organizations and governments do not prioritize initiatives like reskilling programs, retraining opportunities, and policies designed to support displaced workers, the economic divide between high-skill, high-wage, and low-skill, low-wage jobs could grow wider. Additionally, the societal impacts of mass unemployment due to AI-driven automation could strain social welfare systems and create economic instability. Beyond economic concerns, AI also raises ethical issues related to bias and discrimination. AI systems, which often rely on vast datasets to make decisions, can inadvertently perpetuate or even amplify existing societal biases. For example, biased algorithms in hiring software, law enforcement systems, or lending platforms have been shown to reinforce racial, gender, or socioeconomic biases. AI systems are typically trained on historical data, and if that data reflects systemic inequalities, the AI will likely replicate and exacerbate those biases. In the criminal justice system, predictive algorithms used to assess the risk of reoffending have been shown to disproportionately target minority communities, leading to unfair sentencing and parole decisions. Similarly, in hiring practices, AI-based recruitment tools have been found to favor male candidates over female candidates for specific roles or to discriminate against candidates from underrepresented racial groups. The result is that AI, far from being a neutral or objective tool, can deepen existing societal inequalities. Moreover, the lack of transparency in many AI algorithms – often called the "black box" problem – can make it difficult to understand how decisions are made. Without clear accountability, addressing the biases embedded within these systems or preventing them from having harmful real-world consequences is challenging. While AI offers immense opportunities, it also presents significant risks. The automation of jobs, the perpetuation of bias, and the lack of transparency in AI decision-making require careful attention. To ensure that AI benefits society, governments, organizations, and developers must work together to address these challenges, investing in policies and frameworks that promote fairness, accountability, and social responsibility. Only then can the promise of AI be fully realized without amplifying existing societal inequalities.

Technological Advancements in AI Ethics and Security

Artificial Intelligence (AI) is advancing at an extraordinary pace, with new technologies and innovations emerging regularly. This rapid progress promises to bring about transformative changes across various sectors, including healthcare, education, finance, and transportation. However, the increasing capabilities of AI also present a range of complex ethical and security challenges that must be carefully addressed to ensure that these technologies are developed and deployed responsibly. From a technical standpoint, the acceleration of AI is enabling machines to perform tasks that were once thought to be uniquely human. For instance, AI algorithms are now capable of analyzing vast amounts of data, recognizing patterns, and making decisions with an unprecedented level of accuracy. These advancements hold great promise in fields like medical diagnostics, where AI can assist doctors in identifying diseases more efficiently, and in autonomous vehicles, where AI can drive cars with minimal human intervention. While the potential benefits are vast, these innovations also raise significant ethical and security concerns that must be thoughtfully examined. One of the most pressing ethical challenges is ensuring that AI systems are designed and used in a way that is fair and just. As AI increasingly makes decisions that affect people's lives—whether in hiring, lending, healthcare, or law enforcement—there is a real risk that these systems could perpetuate or even amplify existing biases. AI systems often rely on historical data to make predictions and decisions. If this data is biased or reflects societal inequalities, the AI systems can unintentionally replicate and exacerbate those biases. For example, biased algorithms in hiring tools may favor certain demographic groups over others, or predictive policing tools might disproportionately target minority communities, reinforcing systemic discrimination. Therefore, AI development must incorporate diversity, equity, and inclusion principles to mitigate bias and ensure that AI benefits all members of society equally. From a security perspective, the rise of AI brings a host of new vulnerabilities. AI systems, particularly those involved in critical infrastructure like power grids, financial systems, and transportation networks, could become attractive targets for cyberattacks. Malicious actors could exploit weaknesses in AI algorithms or compromise the data that these systems rely on, leading to potentially disastrous consequences. In addition, as AI technologies become more autonomous, ensuring their security against adversarial attacks becomes increasingly challenging. For example, AI-driven autonomous vehicles may be vulnerable to cyberattacks that could disrupt operations or cause accidents. Furthermore, using AI in military applications raises concerns about the risks of AI-driven weapons systems falling into the wrong hands or being used in ways that violate international laws.

Given these challenges, robust ethical frameworks and security protocols must guide the development of AI. This includes creating transparent and accountable systems that allow for the auditing and monitoring of AI decisions and ensuring that AI technologies are designed to prioritize safety, fairness, and privacy. Governments, regulatory bodies, and the private sector must work together to establish clear guidelines and regulations that promote responsible AI development while mitigating the risks of misuse and harm. AI has tremendous potential to improve lives and drive innovation; its rapid advancement requires careful consideration of its ethical and security challenges. Addressing bias, transparency, and security issues will be key to ensuring that AI technologies are developed to benefit society. As AI continues to evolve, technical and ethical considerations must be integrated into its design and deployment to safeguard against unintended consequences and foster a future where AI can be a force for good.

Technological Innovations in AI Ethics

The development of Explainable AI (XAI) is one of the most transformative advancements in AI ethics. Traditional machine learning models, particularly deep learning systems, are often considered "black boxes" because they can make highly accurate predictions or decisions without providing clear insights into the underlying reasoning processes. This lack of transparency can be problematic, especially in high-stakes fields where the consequences of AI decisions are significant. Explainable AI seeks to address this challenge by developing models that are not only effective but also interpretable, ensuring that humans can understand how and why a decision was made. For example, in healthcare, AI systems are increasingly used to assist doctors in diagnosing diseases or recommending treatments. However, if these AI systems are not explainable, healthcare professionals may hesitate to trust their recommendations. By developing AI models that provide clear, understandable reasoning for their suggestions, healthcare providers can ensure that they make informed decisions based on AI recommendations. For example, if an AI system suggests a specific treatment for a patient with a rare condition, an explainable model might provide insights into how the AI arrived at this suggestion, such as by identifying relevant patterns in medical history or test results. This transparency allows doctors to understand better and validate the AI's reasoning, ultimately improving patient outcomes and fostering trust in the system.

Another critical area of advancement in AI ethics is fairness-aware machine learning, which focuses on identifying and reducing biases in AI systems. AI models can inadvertently reinforce or amplify societal biases, such as racial, gender, or socioeconomic, due to skewed training data or biased algorithms. This mainly concerns high-stakes applications such as hiring practices or criminal justice decisions. For example, a biased hiring algorithm might unfairly favor male candidates over female candidates due to the way the system was trained on historical hiring data, which might reflect past gender disparities.

Researchers have developed several techniques to detect and mitigate such biases. Methods like adversarial debiasing, where an algorithm is trained to minimize reliance on sensitive attributes like race or gender, and fair representations, which aim to transform the data to remove these biases, are gaining traction. These techniques ensure that AI systems do not perpetuate or exacerbate societal inequalities. A practical example of fairness-aware machine learning is the development of algorithms used in criminal sentencing. In some instances, AI models have been shown to unfairly predict higher risks of recidivism for minority groups, leading to discriminatory outcomes. By applying fairness techniques, developers aim to reduce biases and ensure that sentencing recommendations are based on relevant, non-discriminatory factors.

AI Security Challenges

Artificial Intelligence (AI) technologies simultaneously enhance and threaten the security landscape. On the one hand, AI-driven cybersecurity tools have become essential for detecting and mitigating cyberattacks in real-time. For example, machine learning (ML) models can analyze enormous datasets to identify patterns and detect anomalous behavior, enabling them to recognize potential security threats before they escalate into full-scale attacks. These AI systems continuously learn from new data, improving their ability to predict and respond to emerging threats. However, the rise of AI also presents new security vulnerabilities. One of the most concerning threats is the weaponization of AI through adversarial attacks. In these attacks, malicious actors manipulate AI models by providing them with specially crafted inputs—often designed to deceive the system into making incorrect decisions. These adversarial inputs can cause AI systems to malfunction in ways that are difficult to detect or predict. For example, an attacker might subtly alter the visual appearance of a stop sign so that an autonomous vehicle's AI misinterprets it as a yield sign, leading to potential accidents. Such vulnerabilities could have profound implications, ranging from the safety of autonomous vehicles to the integrity of financial systems that rely on AI-driven fraud detection algorithms.

In addition to these security risks, AI systems raise significant privacy concerns. Many AI applications require access to vast amounts of personal and sensitive data to function effectively, and this data is often processed and stored in ways that could compromise individuals' privacy. The collection and use of such data necessitate stringent safeguards to prevent unauthorized access and misuse. Techniques such as differential privacy have been developed to help mitigate privacy risks. Differential privacy ensures that individual data points cannot be re-identified within a dataset, even while the data remains valid for analysis. This allows organizations to leverage AI's power while safeguarding individuals' privacy. For example, consider a healthcare AI system that uses patient data to predict medical conditions. While the system can provide valuable insights and improve patient outcomes, it must protect each patient's personal information. Using differential privacy, the system could analyze the data to generate valuable results for researchers and practitioners without revealing personal details about the individuals involved. In sum-up, while AI offers significant advancements in cybersecurity and data analysis, it also introduces new security and privacy challenges that require careful consideration. As AI technology continues to evolve, addressing these challenges will be crucial to ensuring that AI is used responsibly and safely in both private and public sectors.

Predictions for AI Regulation and Policy

As artificial intelligence (AI) technologies continue to advance rapidly, the need for comprehensive regulation has become more urgent. AI systems transform industries from healthcare to finance, education, and transportation, offering vast innovation potential. However, these technologies also raise significant ethical, legal, and social concerns that need to be addressed through robust regulatory frameworks. Governments, international organizations, and policy experts are increasingly aware of the importance of creating guidelines that will facilitate AI's growth, ensure its responsible use, and mitigate the potential risks associated with its deployment. One of the primary concerns driving the call for AI regulation is the potential for harm. AI systems, if misused or left unchecked, can pose serious risks. These risks include the proliferation of biased algorithms, the erosion of privacy, the threat of job displacement, and even the potential for AI to be weaponized. For instance, facial recognition systems have been shown to exhibit racial and gender biases, leading to concerns about unfair treatment and discrimination. Similarly, AI-powered surveillance tools raise privacy concerns, with the potential for abuse by authoritarian governments or malicious actors. In addition, AI systems can automate decisions that affect individuals' lives, such as hiring, lending, or law enforcement, leading to worries about accountability and transparency. To address these challenges, governments worldwide are beginning to implement AI regulations. The European Union (EU) has pioneered AI regulation with its Artificial Intelligence Act, which was introduced in 2021. This landmark legislation aims to establish a comprehensive framework to govern the development and use of AI in Europe, focusing on ensuring safety, transparency, and accountability. The EU's approach categorizes AI applications into different risk levels, from minimal to high risk, and applies specific requirements depending on the level of risk. For example, high-risk AI systems, such as those used in healthcare or transportation, must undergo rigorous testing and certification before deployment. The act also emphasizes the need for human oversight in critical AI applications, ensuring that AI decisions are transparent and can be explained to the public.

Similarly, the United States has begun considering AI regulation, though the approach is more fragmented. States like California have enacted laws around data privacy and AI ethics, while federal agencies, such as the National Institute of Standards and Technology (NIST), are working on guidelines for AI systems' transparency, fairness, and accountability. The U.S. has also seen initiatives like the AI Bill of Rights, which lays out principles for safeguarding civil liberties in an AI-driven society. However, unlike the EU, there is no comprehensive federal AI regulation yet, and debates continue about the best approach.

There is a growing push for global cooperation in AI governance internationally. AI development transcends national borders, and there is a need for coordinated international efforts to ensure consistency in regulation. Organizations like the OECD (Organisation for Economic Cooperation and Development) and the United Nations have discussed creating global frameworks for AI governance, focusing on issues like human rights, safety standards, and ethical guidelines. However, aligning the interests of different countries—especially those with competing technological, economic, and political interests—remains a significant challenge.

In the future, AI regulation will likely become more refined and globally integrated, focusing on balancing innovation with the protection of individuals and society. Policymakers must address emerging issues such as AI explainability, data ownership, ethical decision-making in autonomous systems, and long-term risks associated with advanced AI. The growing role of AI in everyday life also means that public input and collaboration with industry stakeholders will be critical in shaping effective and fair AI regulations. As AI technology evolves, so must the regulatory frameworks that govern it—ensuring that AI's potential is harnessed for the greater good while safeguarding against its risks.

Regulatory Trends in AI

One of the most comprehensive AI regulatory frameworks currently in development is the European Union's Artificial Intelligence Act (AI Act). This groundbreaking legislation classifies AI systems into categories based on their level of risk, ranging from minimal to high risk. High-risk AI systems—such as those used in healthcare, transportation, law enforcement, and critical infrastructure—are subject to more stringent regulations. These include requirements for transparency, accountability, human oversight, and rigorous testing to ensure that the AI systems are safe and ethical. For example, AI tools used in healthcare, like diagnostic algorithms, must undergo a thorough certification process to ensure they meet safety standards and do not cause harm to patients. Similarly, autonomous vehicles and AI-based surveillance systems must adhere to strict rules to mitigate risks to public safety and individual rights. This regulatory approach, emphasizing risk-based classification and ethical principles, is poised to set a global precedent for AI governance, influencing how other countries may approach AI regulation.

In contrast, the United States is still in the process of developing a unified AI regulatory framework. While there is no single comprehensive AI law at the federal level, initiatives like the AI Bill of Rights have emerged to protect individuals' fundamental rights in the face of growing AI use. The Bill of Rights focuses on safeguarding privacy, ensuring non-discrimination, and promoting fairness in AI systems. It also seeks to ensure that AI technologies align with core democratic values like justice, equality, and human dignity. While various states, such as California, have implemented their own regulations, such as the California Consumer Privacy Act (CCPA), federal policymakers are still debating how to approach AI oversight. The fragmented nature of AI regulation in the U.S. reflects the challenge of balancing innovation with the need to protect individuals from potential harm.

As AI regulations become increasingly stringent, organizations worldwide must stay informed about evolving legal frameworks and comply with local and international standards. Since AI technologies are inherently global—often involving data transfer and operations across borders—companies must consider the implications of regulations in their home country and international markets. This will require a proactive approach to understanding and adhering to the varying regulatory requirements of different jurisdictions, ensuring that AI systems are both legally compliant and ethically sound. In this rapidly evolving landscape, staying ahead of regulatory changes will be critical for businesses seeking to build trust with users and avoid legal pitfalls.

Ethical Governance Beyond Compliance

While regulatory frameworks are crucial for managing the risks associated with AI, ethical governance should not be viewed as a mere exercise in compliance. Organizations must take a more proactive approach to AI governance—one that goes beyond meeting the minimum legal requirements. Ethical AI governance involves embedding ethical principles deeply into the organization's culture, policies, and practices, ensuring that AI systems' development and deployment reflect legal standards and broader societal values. A key aspect of this approach is the creation of internal frameworks that address critical ethical concerns such as fairness, accountability, transparency, and privacy. For example, organizations should implement internal policies that ensure AI systems are designed to be fair, meaning they do not discriminate against individuals based on race, gender, or other protected characteristics. AI models should undergo regular audits and testing to identify and mitigate any biases unintentionally introduced during development or training. Accountability is another vital component of ethical governance. Organizations need to establish clear lines of responsibility for AI decision-making, ensuring that both developers and users of AI systems are held accountable for their actions and the outcomes of those systems. This could include creating audit trails to track the decision-making processes of AI systems and implementing mechanisms for addressing errors or unintended consequences that may arise from AI deployment. Transparency is also essential for fostering public trust in AI systems. Organizations should prioritize creating AI systems that are explainable and auditable, meaning non-experts can easily understand their decisions. Providing stakeholders—customers, employees, or the public—with clear and accessible information about how AI systems work and how decisions are made will help build confidence in their fairness and reliability.

Furthermore, organizations should prioritize privacy by ensuring AI systems adhere to the highest data protection standards. This involves implementing safeguards to protect personal and sensitive data and ensuring that AI systems comply with both local and international data protection regulations, such as the General Data Protection Regulation (GDPR) in the European Union.

By adopting a proactive, ethical governance model that goes beyond mere compliance, organizations can demonstrate their commitment to responsible AI development and deployment. This helps mitigate risks and ensures that AI technologies are used in ways that benefit society and promote trust among stakeholders. Ultimately, ethical governance can create long-term value for organizations by fostering innovation that aligns with human rights, fairness, and societal good.

Leadership and Ethics in AI Development

Building an ethical culture in AI development begins with strong, principled leadership. As artificial intelligence continues to evolve and shape industries, ensuring that these technologies are developed and deployed responsibly and ethically is more important than ever. Leadership plays a pivotal role in setting the tone for responsible AI practices, and its influence extends throughout the organization, shaping the values, priorities, and decision-making processes that guide AI development. Ethical leadership is not just about following regulations or compliance standards; it involves creating a culture where ethical considerations are integrated into every stage of the AI lifecycle—from design and development to deployment and beyond. Effective leaders in the AI space must be committed to transparency, fairness, accountability, and inclusivity. This commitment is critical, as AI technologies have the potential to impact society in profound ways, from healthcare to hiring practices, education, criminal justice, and beyond.

A key aspect of ethical leadership in AI is fostering an environment where ethical dilemmas can be openly discussed. Leaders should encourage their teams to think critically about the societal implications of the AI systems they create, asking tough questions about fairness, bias, privacy, and the long-term consequences of these technologies. By establishing open channels for dialogue, leaders empower employees to take responsibility for the ethical outcomes of their work rather than simply following orders or meeting performance metrics.

Moreover, ethical leadership in AI also requires a commitment to diverse perspectives. AI systems are often trained on data that reflects historical biases, which can inadvertently reinforce inequalities if not carefully managed. Leaders who prioritize diversity—both in terms of the teams building AI and the data sets used to train these systems—help ensure that the resulting technology is more likely to be fair, inclusive, and just. Furthermore, strong leadership involves establishing clear guidelines and accountability structures. Ethical principles should be embedded into the organizational framework, with specific measures to assess and address ethical risks throughout development. This includes integrating ethics reviews, audits, and continuous monitoring mechanisms to identify and mitigate any potential harm caused by AI technologies. In conclusion, leadership is at the heart of building an ethical AI culture. By embracing the responsibility of ethical decision-making and fostering an organizational environment that values transparency, inclusivity, and accountability, leaders can guide AI development toward more positive and equitable outcomes for society.

Ethical Leadership in AI

AI development cannot be seen as a purely technical endeavor; it is deeply intertwined with societal values and ethical considerations. Ethical leadership requires executives, managers, and AI developers to consider AI systems' long-term consequences and balance innovation with responsibility.

For example, Satya Nadella, CEO of Microsoft, has consistently emphasized the importance of AI ethics within the company. Under his leadership, Microsoft developed a comprehensive AI ethics framework, including fairness, reliability, privacy, and transparency principles. Nadella's leadership has played a pivotal role in encouraging responsible AI development, signaling to the rest of the tech industry that ethical AI is both a moral and business necessity.

Fostering Ethical AI Development Teams

Ethical leadership also involves fostering diversity in AI teams. Diverse teams are better equipped to identify and address ethical risks because they bring different perspectives. Organizations should prioritize hiring diverse talent—particularly people from underrepresented groups in AI, such as women and minorities—who can help ensure that AI systems serve all of society. Moreover, it is crucial to foster an environment where ethical concerns can be raised without fear of retribution. Organizations should establish clear communication channels for reporting ethical concerns and ensure that leadership takes these concerns seriously.

Creating Ethical Guidelines and Policies for Responsible AI Development

Once leadership has committed to the principles of AI ethics, the next crucial step is to translate this commitment into concrete, actionable guidelines and policies. Developing robust ethical frameworks for AI ensures that artificial intelligence is designed, developed, and deployed in ways that align with societal values, foster trust, and mitigate potential harms. Ethical guidelines and policies are the bedrock upon which responsible AI development is built, providing organizations with the necessary tools to navigate the complexities of AI technology while safeguarding public interests. This section will explore the key components of creating ethical guidelines and policies for AI, including the principles underpinning them, the stakeholders involved in their creation, and the practical considerations for implementing these guidelines across an organization. We will also delve into best practices for fostering an organizational culture of ethical AI development and ensuring that these guidelines remain relevant and effective in the face of technological advancements.

The Importance of Ethical Guidelines and Policies

As AI technology continues to evolve rapidly, its impact on society grows more profound. From autonomous vehicles and healthcare diagnostics to facial recognition systems and predictive policing, AI is becoming integral to a wide array of sectors. However, with this ubiquity comes a range of ethical challenges, such as bias in machine learning algorithms, privacy violations, lack of transparency, and the potential for discrimination. Without clear and comprehensive ethical guidelines, organizations risk inadvertently perpetuating harm, undermining public trust, or facing regulatory and legal consequences. Ethical guidelines and policies serve several critical functions, including:

Establishing a Clear Ethical Framework: Guidelines provide a structured approach to addressing ethical dilemmas and decisions related to AI technology. They help organizations navigate complex issues such as fairness, accountability, and transparency in AI systems.

Mitigating Risk: By implementing policies prioritizing ethical considerations, organizations can avoid harmful outcomes and minimize the risks associated with AI deployment, including legal and reputational risks.

Building Trust and Accountability: A commitment to ethical AI development fosters trust with consumers, stakeholders, and regulatory bodies. Transparent policies prioritizing fairness and accountability can help build public confidence in AI technologies.

Guiding Responsible Innovation: Ethical guidelines help organizations balance the drive for innovation with the need to protect fundamental rights, ensuring that technological advancements align with societal well-being.

Key Principles for Ethical AI

The development of ethical AI guidelines begins with defining the principles that will guide AI development and deployment. These principles should reflect the organization's core values and address key ethical challenges associated with AI.

While there is no universal consensus on these principles' precise wording or structure, several frameworks have emerged over the past few years that provide useful reference points.

Fairness

Fairness is one of the most critical principles in AI ethics. AI systems can inadvertently perpetuate or amplify biases in data, leading to discriminatory outcomes. This is particularly concerning in areas such as hiring, lending, law enforcement, and healthcare, where biased algorithms can profoundly affect people's lives.

Fairness in AI requires the development of algorithms that do not discriminate based on race, gender, age, disability, or other protected characteristics. This may involve ensuring that datasets used to train AI models represent diverse populations and that algorithms are rigorously tested to identify and mitigate bias.

Several approaches to fairness in AI have been proposed, including:

- **Individual Fairness**: Ensuring that similar individuals receive similar treatment from AI systems.
- **Group Fairness**: Ensuring AI decisions do not disproportionately harm or benefit specific demographic groups.
- **Fairness through Transparency**: Providing clear explanations of how AI models make decisions, enabling individuals to understand why they were treated in a particular way.

Accountability

It is essential to ensure that AI systems are deployed responsibly and that organizations take ownership of their AI's behavior and outcomes. This includes establishing clear lines of responsibility for designing, developing, and using AI systems. Accountability can be achieved through various mechanisms, such as:

- **Clear Governance Structures**: Defining roles and responsibilities within an organization for overseeing AI projects and ensuring that ethical considerations are integrated at every stage of development.
- **Audits and Impact Assessments**: Conduct regular audits and risk assessments to evaluate the impact of AI systems, particularly in high-stakes applications.
- **Human-in-the-Loop Systems**: Ensuring that human agents can monitor and override AI decisions, when necessary, particularly in sensitive domains like healthcare or criminal justice.

Transparency

It involves making AI systems understandable and accessible to all stakeholders. This includes explaining AI-driven decisions and ensuring that individuals can understand how AI systems use their data.

There are different types of transparency that organizations should consider:

- **Algorithmic Transparency**: Providing insight into how AI algorithms work, including the logic behind their decision-making processes, and offering users the ability to challenge decisions.
- **Data Transparency**: Ensure that the data used to train AI models is accessible and understandable so stakeholders can assess its quality and fairness.
- **Process Transparency**: Offering visibility into the development and deployment processes, including the measures taken to ensure that ethical standards are upheld.

Privacy and Data Protection

AI systems often rely on large datasets, including personal, sensitive, or confidential information. It is crucial to prioritize data privacy and protection throughout the AI development lifecycle.

Organizations should adhere to the following principles to safeguard privacy:

- **Data Minimization**: Collecting only the data necessary for the AI system to function effectively.
- **Informed Consent**: Obtaining explicit consent from individuals whose data is being used by AI systems, ensuring they understand how their data will be processed.
- **Data Anonymization**: Where possible, anonymizing data to reduce the risk of misuse or unauthorized access.
- **Compliance with Regulations**: Adhering to data protection regulations such as the General Data Protection Regulation (GDPR) and the California Consumer Privacy Act (CCPA).

Safety and Security

AI systems must be designed to operate safely and securely, minimizing the risk of harm to users or society. This includes ensuring that AI systems are resilient to attacks, vulnerabilities, and failures.

Key considerations for safety and security in AI include:

- **Robustness**: Ensuring that AI systems perform reliably in various conditions and can handle unforeseen scenarios without causing harm.
- **Security**: Implementing safeguards to protect AI systems from cyberattacks or malicious manipulation, particularly in critical applications like autonomous vehicles or healthcare.
- **Continuous Monitoring**: Regularly monitor AI systems to identify potential risks or failures and implement corrective measures.

Beneficence and non-maleficence

AI systems should aim to benefit society while minimizing harm. This principle emphasizes that AI should enhance human well-being and avoid causing negative social, economic, or environmental consequences.

Organizations should assess the potential benefits and risks of AI applications through:

- **Ethical Impact Assessments**: Conduct thorough assessments to identify AI systems' potential harms and unintended consequences before deployment.
- **Social Good**: Ensuring AI applications align with broader societal goals, promoting equality, environmental sustainability, and public health.

Inclusivity

Inclusivity ensures that AI systems are accessible and beneficial to all individuals, regardless of their background, socioeconomic status, or abilities. This principle advocates for reducing inequalities and ensuring that AI benefits are equitably distributed.

Organizations can promote inclusivity by:

- **Diverse Teams**: Building AI development teams that reflect various perspectives and experiences, ensuring that different needs and viewpoints are considered.
- **Accessibility**: Designing AI systems accessible to people with disabilities and those in underserved communities.
- **Global Perspective**: Considering the global impact of AI systems, particularly in healthcare, education, and social services, to ensure that AI technologies benefit a wide range of populations.

Developing AI Ethical Guidelines and Policies

Once the core ethical principles have been defined, organizations must translate them into practical guidelines and policies that can be followed by all stakeholders involved in the development and deployment of AI systems. Creating these guidelines should be collaborative, transparent, and inclusive, involving input from various stakeholders, including developers, ethicists, legal experts, and affected communities.

Engage Stakeholders Early

Engaging key stakeholders early in the process of developing ethical AI guidelines is

essential. This includes not only AI developers and data scientists but also ethicists, legal experts, and representatives from marginalized or impacted communities. By fostering a multidisciplinary approach, organizations can ensure that their guidelines reflect a wide range of perspectives and are better equipped to address diverse ethical challenges.
Stakeholders should be involved in:

- **Needs Assessment**: Identifying the ethical concerns and risks associated with AI applications in specific contexts.
- **Drafting Guidelines**: Collaboratively drafting policies and guidelines that align with the organization's ethical principles.
- **Feedback and Revision**: Ensuring that the guidelines are subject to review and refinement based on input from stakeholders.

Incorporate Ethics into the AI Lifecycle

Ethical considerations should not be an afterthought; they should be integrated into every stage of the AI lifecycle, from data collection and algorithm design to deployment and ongoing monitoring. This approach, often called "ethics by design," ensures that AI systems are developed with ethics at the forefront.
Organizations should:

- **Conduct Ethical Risk Assessments**: Before starting any AI project, assess the potential ethical risks and implications, including fairness, privacy, security, and societal impact.
- **Implement Ethical Review Processes**: Establish ethical review boards or committees to oversee the development process and ensure ethical guidelines are followed.
- **Monitor and Audit AI Systems**: Continuously monitor AI systems post-deployment to assess their real-world impact and adjust as necessary.

Create a Framework for Compliance

Ethical guidelines and policies need to be enforceable. Organizations should establish precise mechanisms for ensuring compliance, including:

- **Training and Education**: Provide ongoing training for employees and stakeholders to ensure they understand and can apply ethical guidelines.
- **Audit and Reporting Mechanisms**: Implement regular audits of AI systems to ensure they comply with ethical standards. Encourage transparency and accountability through reporting mechanisms that allow employees and users to flag ethical concerns.
- **Disciplinary Measures**: Develop protocols for addressing violations of ethical guidelines, including corrective actions and sanctions when necessary.

Ensure Continuous Improvement

AI is rapidly evolving, and ethical guidelines must evolve alongside technological advancements. To ensure that ethical policies remain relevant and practical, organizations should establish a process for continuous review and improvement of their AI ethics guidelines.
This includes:

- **Regular Reviews**: Review and update AI ethics guidelines to address new challenges, emerging risks, and evolving societal values.
- **Feedback Loops**: Create mechanisms for gathering feedback from users, stakeholders, and external experts to identify areas for improvement.
- **Adaptation to Legal and Regulatory Changes**: Stay abreast of new laws and regulations related to AI and data privacy and adjust policies accordingly.

Foster a Culture of Ethical AI Development

Ultimately, the success of AI ethics guidelines and policies depends on the organizational culture. Leaders must foster a culture that prioritizes ethical decision-making at every level of the organization. This requires:

- **Leadership Commitment**: Senior leaders should actively champion AI ethics and lead by example, setting a tone that ethics are integral to the organization's mission and values.
- **Employee Empowerment**: Encourage employees to voice concerns about ethical issues and provide them with the tools and support they need to make ethical decisions.
- **Ethical Innovation**: Promote a mindset where innovation is encouraged but balanced with a strong commitment to ethical responsibility.

Creating ethical guidelines and policies for AI is an essential step for ensuring responsible AI development and a powerful tool for building public trust and promoting positive societal outcomes. By establishing clear, actionable principles and integrating them into the AI lifecycle, organizations can ensure that their AI systems are developed and deployed in ways that prioritize fairness, accountability, transparency, privacy, and safety. As AI continues to shape the future of technology and society, organizations must take a proactive approach to ethical decision-making. Developing robust AI ethics guidelines and policies is necessary for achieving this goal. By doing so, organizations can help ensure that AI remains a force for good, driving innovation while safeguarding the values essential for a just and equitable society.

Measuring and Evaluating Ethical AI Performance

To ensure that ethical guidelines are being effectively implemented and adhered to, organizations must establish robust mechanisms for measuring and evaluating the ethical performance of their AI systems. Without continuous monitoring and evaluation, it is impossible to determine whether AI systems are fulfilling their intended ethical goals, such as fairness, transparency, accountability, and privacy protection. Regular assessments allow organizations to identify potential ethical issues, rectify them before they become significant problems, and continuously improve the design and deployment of AI technologies.

The evaluation process should begin by defining clear and measurable ethical standards, which can be linked to the organization's overarching AI policies. These standards may cover a range of ethical concerns, including bias detection, algorithmic transparency, data privacy, and the social impact of AI systems. Once these standards are established, organizations can employ various tools and methodologies to assess whether their AI systems align with these principles.

For example, regular audits of AI models can help detect biases in training data or algorithmic decision-making processes that may result in unfair outcomes. Fairness metrics, such as disparate impact analysis or individual fairness evaluations, can be used to assess whether AI systems treat all demographic groups equitably. Additionally, transparency evaluations, such as model explainability checks, can ensure that AI decisions are understandable and can be explained to stakeholders, helping to build trust and accountability. Another critical aspect of evaluating ethical AI performance is conducting impact assessments to examine the broader societal implications of AI systems. These assessments may involve examining the potential risks AI poses to vulnerable populations, the environment, or global social equity. Furthermore, ongoing feedback from stakeholders—including users, affected communities, and external experts—should be actively sought and incorporated into the evaluation process. By continuously measuring and evaluating AI systems' ethical performance, organizations can ensure they are aligned with their ethical commitments, minimize risks, and maximize the positive societal impact of their AI technologies.

Bias Detection and Mitigation

AI systems can inadvertently perpetuate biases if they are not carefully monitored. Organizations should implement bias detection tools to identify and mitigate potential biases in AI models. For instance, tools like Fairness Flow and AI Fairness 360 can help detect disparities in how different demographic groups are treated by AI systems.

Ethical Audits

Conducting regular ethical audits is a key part of AI governance. These audits review AI systems to ensure they align with ethical guidelines and regulatory requirements. Audits should focus on data fairness, algorithm transparency, and accountability and involve external stakeholders, such as independent ethics experts, to ensure impartiality.

Performance Metrics for Ethical AI

To measure ethical performance, organizations should develop specific metrics. These might include:

- **Fairness metrics**: Measuring whether an AI system produces equitable user outcomes.
- **Transparency metrics**: Assessing the explainability of AI decisions.
- **Accountability metrics**: Evaluating the extent to which AI systems allow human oversight and intervention.

By systematically evaluating these factors, organizations can ensure that their AI systems operate ethically and responsibly.

Conclusion

Building an ethical AI culture within organizations is not just a best practice but an imperative for navigating AI development's complex and often unpredictable challenges. As AI technologies evolve, a strong ethical foundation becomes even more critical. Organizations must remain proactive in understanding emerging trends, preparing for regulatory changes, and fostering an environment where ethical considerations are integrated into every stage of AI development. This involves more than simply adhering to current ethical standards—it requires anticipating the social, economic, and environmental impacts that AI may have in the future and developing frameworks that can adapt to these challenges.Ethical leadership plays a central role in setting the tone for AI development. Leaders must endorse ethical principles and embed them into the organization's mission, culture, and operations. By creating clear policies, investing in education and training, and ensuring all stakeholders are involved in ethical decision-making, organizations can cultivate a workforce equipped to address AI's ethical dilemmas thoughtfully and effectively. Additionally, robust evaluation mechanisms, such as regular audits and impact assessments, must ensure that AI systems function as intended and do not perpetuate harm or discrimination. Committing to ethical AI development ultimately strengthens public trust, which is essential for these technologies' widespread adoption and acceptance. By prioritizing fairness, transparency, and accountability, organizations mitigate risks and enhance their reputation as responsible innovators. In doing so, they contribute to a future where AI is a powerful tool for positive social change, improving lives, and promoting justice, equity, and human well-being. Therefore, Ethical AI development is not merely a legal or operational necessity but a moral imperative for ensuring that technology truly benefits society.

Appendix-A

Glossary

Core AI and Applications

1. **AI** - Artificial Intelligence
2. **ARIMA** - Autoregressive Integrated Moving Average
3. **CNN** - Convolutional Neural Network
4. **GAN** - Generative Adversarial Network
5. **GenAI** - Generative Artificial Intelligence
6. **GPT** - Generative Pre-trained Transformer
7. **GPU** - Graphics Processing Unit
8. **LLM** - Large Language Model
9. **LIME** - Local Interpretable Model-Agnostic Explanations
10. **LSTM** - Long Short-Term Memory
11. **ML** - Machine Learning
12. **NLP** - Natural Language Processing
13. **OCR** - Optical Character Recognition
14. **RNN** - Recurrent Neural Network
15. **SHAP** - SHapley Additive exPlanations
16. **TPU** - Tensor Processing Unit
17. **VAE** - Variational Autoencoder
18. **XAI** - Explainable Artificial Intelligence

AI Security and Governance

1. **ACID** - Atomicity, Consistency, Isolation, Durability
2. **APTs** - Advanced Persistent Threats
3. **CSRF** - Cross-Site Request Forgery
4. **DDoS** - Distributed Denial of Service
5. **DoS** - Denial of Service

6. **DR & BC** - Disaster Recovery and Business Continuity
7. **EDR** - Endpoint Detection and Response
8. **HIPAA** - Health Insurance Portability and Accountability Act
9. **IDS** - Intrusion Detection System
10. **MFA** - Multi-Factor Authentication
11. **MitM** - Man-in-the-Middle
12. **OWASP** - Open Web Application Security Project
13. **PCI DSS** - Payment Card Industry Data Security Standard
14. **RBAC** - Role-Based Access Control
15. **SHA-256** - Secure Hash Algorithm 256-bit
16. **SSO** - Single Sign-On
17. **SSRF** - Server-Side Request Forgery
18. **TLS** - Transport Layer Security
19. **VPN** - Virtual Private Network
20. **XSS** - Cross-Site Scripting

Ethical AI and Global Governance

1. **AIDA** - Artificial Intelligence and Data Act
2. **CCPA** - California Consumer Privacy Act
3. **GAIA** - Global AI Action Alliance
4. **GDPR** - General Data Protection Regulation
5. **GPAI** - Global Partnership on Artificial Intelligence
6. **ISO** - International Organization for Standardization
7. **PIPL** - Personal Information Protection Law
8. **ERM** - Enterprise Risk Management

International and Regional Organizations

1. **APEC** - Asia-Pacific Economic Cooperation
2. **AU** - African Union
3. **EU** - European Union
4. **FDA** - Food and Drug Administration
5. **G7** - Group of Seven
6. **G20** - Group of Twenty
7. **IEC** - International Electrotechnical Commission
8. **ITU** - International Telecommunication Union
9. **OECD** - Organization for Economic Co-operation and Development
10. **UNESCO** - United Nations Educational, Scientific, and Cultural Organization
11. **WEF** - World Economic Forum

Commonly used AI and Security Terms for Quick Reference

AI Terms

1. **Adversarial Attacks** - Manipulating input data to deceive AI models.
2. **Adversarial Learning** - Improving AI robustness by exposing models to malicious or challenging inputs during training.
3. **Adversarial Robustness** - The ability of AI systems to withstand malicious inputs or attacks.
4. **Agentic AI** - AI systems automating complex workflows with decision-making capabilities.
5. **Algorithmic Fairness** - Ensuring AI decisions are equitable across different demographic groups.
6. **ARIMA Models** - Statistical models for analyzing and forecasting time series data by combining autoregression, differencing, and moving averages.
7. **Autoencoders** - Neural networks used for encoding and reconstructing data efficiently in unsupervised learning.
8. **Bias** - Systematic errors in AI outputs due to skewed training data or flawed

algorithm design.

9. **Bias Detection** - Identifying and mitigating biases in AI models to ensure fairness.

10. **Bias Mitigation** - Techniques to reduce or eliminate unfair biases in AI systems.

11. **Black Box Problem** - Lack of transparency in AI models, making it difficult to understand how decisions are made.

12. **Computer Vision** - AI that enables machines to interpret and analyze visual data like images and videos.

13. **Data Privacy** - Protecting personal data from misuse or unauthorized access in AI systems.

14. **Deep Learning** - An advanced ML technique using neural networks with many layers to model complex patterns in large datasets.

15. **Diffusion Models** - Generative models refining random noise into realistic data like images or text.

16. **Differential Privacy** - Adding noise to data to preserve individual privacy while enabling aggregated insights.

17. **Dynamic Pricing** - AI-driven pricing strategies that adjust prices in real-time based on demand and competition.

18. **Ethical AI** - AI systems developed and deployed to align with human rights and societal values.

19. **Ethical Governance** - Frameworks ensuring AI aligns with ethical principles like fairness and accountability.

20. **Ethical Impact Assessment** - Evaluations of the societal implications of AI technologies.

21. **Ethical Testing** - Assessing AI for fairness, bias, and compliance with ethical norms.

22. **Explainability** - Making AI decisions understandable and transparent to users.

23. **Explainable AI (XAI)** - AI systems designed to provide clear insights into decision-making processes.

24. **Fairness** - Ensuring AI systems treat all groups impartially and without discrimination.
25. **Fairness-Aware Machine Learning** - Techniques to identify and mitigate biases in AI models.
26. **Facial Recognition** - AI technology to identify and verify individuals based on facial features.
27. **Generative AI** - AI systems that generate new content like text, images, or music based on learned patterns.
28. **Governance Testing** - Validating adherence to legal and accountability frameworks.
29. **Human-in-the-Loop (HITL)** - A model where humans oversee and control AI decisions in critical processes.
30. **Limited Memory AI** - AI systems that use past experiences or data temporarily to make decisions, such as autonomous vehicles.
31. **Machine Learning (ML)** - A subset of AI that enables machines to learn from data and improve their performance over time without explicit programming.
32. **Model Drift** - Degradation of AI model accuracy over time due to unseen data.
33. **Model Interpretability** - Understanding the logic behind AI model decisions.
34. **Named Entity Recognition (NER)** - NLP techniques to identify and classify entities like names, locations, or organizations in text.
35. **Natural Language Processing (NLP)** - AI that focuses on the interaction between computers and human language, enabling tasks like translation and text analysis.
36. **Neural Networks** - Computational models inspired by the human brain, consisting of interconnected nodes (neurons) that process information.
37. **Optimization Algorithm** - Techniques used to find the best solution to a problem, such as minimizing costs or maximizing efficiency.
38. **Pruning** - A model optimization technique to remove less significant parameters in neural networks for efficiency.
39. **Quantization** - Reducing the precision of model computations to improve

performance and reduce resource usage.

40. **Recommender Systems** - AI systems that suggest items or content to users based on their preferences and behavior.
41. **Reinforcement Learning** - Training AI models based on reward feedback.
42. **Scenario-Based Testing** - Simulating real-world conditions to evaluate AI performance.
43. **Self-Aware AI** - A hypothetical AI with self-consciousness, understanding its own existence, emotions, and thoughts.
44. **Speech-to-Text/Text-to-Speech** - AI systems that convert spoken language into text and vice versa.
45. **Strong AI (General AI)** - A theoretical AI possessing general intelligence to perform tasks across various domains without human intervention.
46. **Super AI (Artificial Superintelligence)** - A hypothetical AI surpassing human intelligence and capabilities in virtually every field.
47. **Supervised Learning** - ML where the model is trained on labeled data to make predictions or classifications.
48. **Sustainable AI** - Developing AI with minimal environmental impact, often referred to as "Green AI."
49. **Theory of Mind AI** - A theoretical AI capable of understanding emotions, beliefs, and intentions of others.
50. **Timeseries Analysis** - Techniques to analyze and forecast data points collected over time, such as stock prices or weather patterns.
51. **Transparency** - The clarity in AI systems regarding their operations, data usage, and decision-making processes.
52. **Trustworthy AI** - AI systems designed with principles of fairness, transparency, accountability, and inclusivity.
53. **Unsupervised Learning** - ML that identifies hidden patterns in data without predefined labels or categories.
54. **Variational Autoencoders (VAEs)** - A type of autoencoder used for generating new data and detecting anomalies.
55. **Weak AI (Narrow AI)** - AI designed to perform a specific task efficiently but

lacks general intelligence or adaptability outside its predefined scope.

Security Terms

1. **Access Control** - Restricting system access based on roles and permissions.
2. **Continuous Monitoring** - Regularly evaluating AI systems to maintain performance and security.
3. **Cybersecurity for AI** - Measures to protect AI systems from threats like adversarial inputs and data breaches.
4. **Data Integrity** - Ensuring data accuracy and consistency during storage and processing.
5. **Denial of Service (DoS)** - Overloading systems to disrupt services.
6. **Encryption** - Securing data by converting it into a coded format.
7. **Endpoint Security** - Protecting devices like laptops and mobile phones from threats.
8. **Insider Threats** - Security risks posed by individuals within an organization.
9. **Malware** - Malicious software like viruses or ransomware.
10. **Penetration Testing** - Simulating attacks to identify vulnerabilities in AI systems.
11. **Phishing** - Deceptive attacks to steal sensitive information.
12. **Robustness** - The ability of AI systems to operate reliably under diverse and unforeseen conditions.
13. **Security Testing** - Assessing AI systems for vulnerabilities and fortifying defenses.
14. **Threat Modeling** - Identifying potential security risks during system design.
15. **Zero-Trust Architecture -** Assuming all users and devices are untrusted by default.

Notes Date: